101
FUN WARM-UP AND COOL-DOWN GAMES

101
FUN WARM-UP AND COOL-DOWN GAMES

John Byl

Human Kinetics

Library of Congress Cataloging-in-Publication Data

Byl, John.
    101 fun warm-up and cool-down games / John Byl.
        p. cm.
Includes bibliographical references.
    ISBN 0-7360-4849-9 (softcover)
    1. Exercise for children. 2. Physical education for children. 3.
Group games. I. Title: One hundred one fun warm-up and cool-down games.
II. Title: One hundred and one fun warm-up and cool-down games. III.
Title.
    GV443.B94 2004
    613.7'1--dc21
                                              2003012252

ISBN-10: 0-7360-4849-9
ISBN-13: 978-0-7360-4849-1

Copyright © 2004 by John Byl

Acquisitions Editor: Gayle Kassing, PhD; **Developmental Editor:** Melissa Feld; **Assistant Editor:** Susan C. Hagan; **Copyeditor:** Bob Replinger; **Proofreader:** Julie Marx Goodreau; **Permission Manager:** Dalene Reeder; **Graphic Designer:** Andrew Tietz; **Graphic Artist:** Dawn Sills; **Photo Manager:** Kareema McLendon; **Cover Designer:** Andrea Souflée; **Photographer (cover and interior):** Darren Lampson; **Art Manager:** Kelly Hendren; **Illustrator:** Craig Newsom; **Printer:** United Graphics

We thank Redeemer University College in Ancaster, Ontario, for assistance in providing the location for the photo shoot for this book. The following games are illustrated:

On the cover: Under Frog; Chapter 1: Running the Rails; Chapter 2: Balance Tag; Chapter 3: Custodian Relay; Chapter 4: Le Mans 24-Lap Tandem Race; Chapter 5: Under Frog; Chapter 6: Cooperative Net Play; Chapter 7: Jog Toss; Chapter 8: Pass Around; Chapter 9: Round the Corners Snap; Chapter 10: Obstacle Course for Hockey; Chapter 11: Split Triangle Run; Chapter 12: Frozen Tag

Printed in the United States of America   10   9   8   7   6   5   4   3

Human Kinetics
Web site: www.HumanKinetics.com

United States: Human Kinetics
P.O. Box 5076
Champaign, IL 61825-5076
800-747-4457
e-mail: humank@hkusa.com

Canada: Human Kinetics
475 Devonshire Road Unit 100
Windsor, ON N8Y 2L5
800-465-7301 (in Canada only)
e-mail: orders@hkcanada.com

Europe: Human Kinetics
107 Bradford Road
Stanningley
Leeds LS28 6AT, United Kingdom
+44 (0) 113 255 5665
e-mail: hk@hkeurope.com

Australia: Human Kinetics
57A Price Avenue
Lower Mitcham, South Australia 5062
08 8277 1555
e-mail: liaw@hkaustralia.com

New Zealand: Human Kinetics
Division of Sports Distributors NZ Ltd.
P.O. Box 300 226 Albany
North Shore City
Auckland
0064 9 448 1207
e-mail: info@humankinetics.co.nz

I dedicate this book to Pat Doyle, who contributed
more to encouraging fun, active participation for
kids in Canada than anyone I know. Thanks, Pat!

I have come that they may have life,
and have it to the full.
John 10:10

CONTENTS

PART II SPORT-SPECIFIC WARM-UP AND COOL-DOWN GAMES

GAME FINDER

This game finder is meant to help you quickly find the right games. If you remember the name of the game, you can find it easily because all games are listed alphabetically. All games are numbered in the text from game 1 to game 101. Game variations are indicated with a "v." For example, game 7 is Swamp Monster. Game 7v, Eliminating Swamp Monsters, is a variation of game 7. The number of players recommended for each game is also listed. For any game, leaders can divide a large number of players into several teams so that all can participate. For example, if a game is best suited for 4 to 8 players and the leader has 24 players, the group can be divided into three to six teams to include everyone.

The Experience column identifies the amount of experience helpful to perform the game. If anyone from a novice to an expert can play the game, the experience level is listed as "All." If some experience is helpful the game is identified with "Experienced," and games requiring a high degree of skill are identified with "Expert." The playing area describes the basic surface or facility needs of the game. The Sport column identifies whether the game can be used in a variety of sports or is especially suited to a specific sport. If the Sport column has the word "Most" in it, then the game will work well as a general warm-up for most sports. Games that are sport specific usually require specialized skills and equipment. The last column indicates whether the game is appropriate as a cool-down.

KEY

Badminton		Hockey	
Baseball		Soccer	
Basketball		Volleyball	
Football		Cool-Down	

Game number	Game	Page number	Number of players	Experience	Playing area	Sport	Cool-Down
90	2-4 Keep-Away	154	2 teams of 3-4	Experienced	Any flat surface		
79	3-on-2 Keep-Away	137	Groups of 5-10	Experienced	Ice surface		
24	Arch and Roll Relay	45	Teams of 5-15	All	Any flat surface	Most	
30v	Backward Butt Crawl	53	Teams of 3-8	All	Any flat surface	Most	
26v	Backward Heel-to-Toe Race	48	Any number	All	Any flat surface	Most	
33v	Backward Over, Under, and Around	57	Teams of 3	All	Any smooth floor	Most	
18	Balance Tag	36	Any number	All	Any flat surface	Most	
18v	Balance Any Tag	36	Any number	All	Any flat surface	Most	
14	Ball Safe	32	Groups of 5-15	All	Any flat surface	Most	
95	Balloon Volleyball	164	12 or more	Experienced	Volleyball court		
3v	Base Runners	18	Teams of 4-8	Experienced	Open space		
90v	Basketball Pass 2-4 Keep-Away	155	2 teams of 3-4	Experienced	Any flat surface		
42v	Bird Catcher	73	1	Experienced	Any flat surface		
42v	Bird Flick	73	1	Experienced	Any flat surface		
42	Bird Juggle	72	1	Experienced	Any flat surface		
42v	Bird Trap	72	1	Experienced	Any flat surface		
16v	Blinders Island Tag	34	Groups of 10 or more	All	Any flat surface	Most	
21	Blindfolded Obstacle Relay	41	Teams of 3	All	Any flat surface	Most	
43v	Broken Buttonhole	75	Teams of 5-8	Experienced	Half a badminton court		
30	Butt Crawl	53	Teams of 3-8	All	Any smooth floor	Most	
43v	Buttonhole	75	Teams of 5-8	Experienced	Half a badminton court		

x

Game number	Game	Page number	Number of players	Experience	Playing area	Sport	Cool-Down
43v	Buttonhole Sit-up	75	Teams of 5-8	Experienced	Half a badminton court		
50v	Cat Badminton	89	3	Expert	Badminton court without a net		
50	Cat in the Middle	88	3	Expert	Badminton court without a net		
29v	Caterpillar Bend	52	Teams of 3-15	All	Any flat surface	Most	
29	Caterpillar Race	52	Teams of 3-15	All	Any flat surface	Most	
19	Circle Relay	38	Teams of 5-8	All	Any flat surface	Most	
19v	Circle Weave	39	Teams of 5-8	All	Any flat surface	Most	
28v	Circular Everybody Over and Under	51	Teams of 4-10	All	Any flat surface	Most	
44	Clear, Drop	76	Partners	Experienced	Badminton court		
49v	Competitive Net Game	87	2	Experienced	Badminton court		
49v	Competitive Two-Zone Net Game	87	2	Experienced	Badminton court		
74	Completed Passes	127	Teams of 6-12	Experienced	Any flat field		
12v	Continuous Basketball British Bulldog	30	Any number	All	Any flat surface		
12	Continuous British Bulldog	30	Any number	All	Any flat surface	Most	
27v	Continuous Over and Under	50	Teams of 5-10	All	Gymnasium or large room	Most	
101	Continuous Pass	176	12 or more	Expert	Volleyball court		
9	Continuous Scooter Tag	26	Any number	All	Any flat surface	Most	
9v	Continuous Scooter Dribble Tag	26	Any number	All	Any flat surface		
49	Cooperative Net Game	86	2	Experienced	Badminton court		
82	Crazy Eights	144	Any number	All	Any flat surface		

Game number	Game	Page number	Number of players	Experience	Playing area	Sport	Cool-Down
20	Cumulative Relay	40	Teams of 3-6	All	Any flat surface	Most	
23v	Custodial Wheels	44	Teams of 2-4	All	Open area with a hard, slippery floor (gymnasium, hallway)	Most	
23	Custodian Relay	44	Teams of 2-4	All	Open area with a hard, slippery floor (gymnasium, hallway)	Most	
10	Dog's Tail	27	Teams of 5-10	All	Any flat surface	Most	
81	Double-Up	140	Teams of 2-8	Experienced	Ice surface		
86	Double Cone Ball	148	Pairs	All	Any flat surface		
71v	Double Name Calling Hot Football	122	Groups of 7-15	All	Any flat surface		
6v	Double Track	21	Groups of 5 or more	All	Any flat surface	Most	
44v	Doubles Clear, Drop	77	2 pairs	Experienced	Badminton court		
45v	Doubles Long Cross and Drop	79	2 pairs	Experienced	Badminton court		
49v	Doubles Net Game	87	2 pairs	Experienced	Badminton court		
52v	Doubles Short, Long, and Wide	92	2 pairs	Expert	Badminton court		
48v	Doubles Upset	84	At least 6 per court	Experienced	Badminton court		
18v	Dribble Balance Tag	36	Any number	All	Any flat surface		
19v	Dribble Circle Relay	39	Teams of 5-8	All	Any flat surface		
66	Dribble Tag	113	Any number	Experienced	Any flat surface		

Game number	Game	Page number	Number of players	Experience	Playing area	Sport	Cool-Down
88	Dribble Goal Line	150	Teams of 3	Experienced	Any flat surface	⚽	🌀
66v	Dribble Tag the Ball	113	Any number	Experienced	Any flat surface	🏀	🌀
51	Driving	90	Pairs	Expert	Badminton court	🏸	
7v	Eliminating Swamp Monsters	22	Any number	All	Any flat surface	Most	🌀
69v	Elimination Bump	118	5-50	Experienced	A basketball court with several baskets marked with free-throw lines	🏀	🌀
28	Everybody Over and Under	51	Teams of 4-10	All	Any flat surface	Most	🌀
19v	Everyone Goes	39	Teams of 5-8	All	Any flat surface	Most	
17	Everyone It Frozen Tag	35	Any number	All	Any flat surface	Most	🌀
25	Exercise Relay	46	Teams of 5-8	All	Any flat surface	Most	
99	Five-Pass Volleyball	172	2 teams of 6	Expert	Volleyball court	🏐	🌀
47	Five-Player Continuous Rally	82	At least 5	Experienced	Badminton court	🏸	🌀
13	Flusher	31	Any number	All	Any flat surface	Most	🌀
4	Follow the Leader	19	Any size group	All	A gymnasium floor with lines	Most 🏀🏒⚽	🌀
97v	Forearm Threes	169	Groups of 3	Experienced	Volleyball court	🏐	🌀
51v	Four-Wheel Driving	90	2 pairs	Expert	Badminton court	🏸	
55v	Fowl Throw	97	Groups of 5 or more	All	Any flat surface	🏏	🌀
32v	Frogs and Snakes	56	Teams of 3-13	All	Any flat surface	Most	🌀
32v	Front Crawl	55	Teams of 3-13	All	Any flat surface	Most	🌀

Game number	Game	Page number	Number of players	Experience	Playing area	Sport	Cool-Down
3	Front of the Class	17	Teams of 4-8	Experienced	Open space	Most	
3v	Front of the Sport Dribble Class	18	Teams of 4-8	Experienced	Open space		
98v	Frozen Ball Tag	171	Groups of 6 or more	Experienced	Volleyball court		
98	Frozen Tag	170	Groups of 6 or more	Experienced	Volleyball court		
89	Grid Pass	152	Groups of 4	Experienced	Any flat surface		
91v	Group Juggle	156	2-5	Experienced	Open space		
49v	Half Cooperative Net Game	87	2	Experienced	Badminton court		
26	Heel-to-Toe Race	48	Any number	All	Any flat surface	Most	
1	High Fives	14	Teams of 5-35	All	Any flat surface	Most	
41	High Rollers	68	Teams of 5-25	All	Any flat surface	Most	
77	Hockey Soccer	133	Teams of 3-5	Experienced	Ice surface		
34	Hole in One	58	Teams of 7 or more	All	Any flat surface	Most	
60	Hot Box	103	Teams of 3	Experienced	Any flat field		
71	Hot Football	122	Groups of 7-15	All	Any flat surface		
71v	Hot Footballs	122	Groups of 7-15	All	Any flat surface		
58	Hot Potato Baseball	100	Teams of 3-8	Experienced	Any flat surface		
94v	I Spy Shower Volleyball	163	2 teams of 6 or more	Experienced	Volleyball court		
16	Island Tag	34	Groups of 10 or more	All	Any flat surface	Most	
55v	Jog Double Toss	96	Groups of 5 or more	All	Any flat surface		
55v	Jog Forward Toss	96	Groups of 5 or more	All	Any flat surface		
55	Jog Toss	96	Groups of 5 or more	All	Any flat surface		

Game number	Game	Page number	Number of players	Experience	Playing area	Sport	Cool-Down
91	Jugglers	156	1	Experienced	Open space		
63v	Kick to a Wall Relay	109	Teams of 3	All	Any flat surface with a wall		
15	Knee Tag	33	Any number of pairs	All	Any flat surface	Most	
80v	Lane Two-Line Pass	139	Groups of 5-10	Experienced	Ice surface		
38	Le Mans 24-Lap Tandem Race	63	Teams of 3	Experienced	Any floor	Most	
37	Leapfrog	61	Teams of 2	Experienced	Any flat surface	Most	
37v	Leapfrog, Leapfrog, Octopus, Octopus	61	Teams of 2	Experienced	Any flat surface	Most	
37v	Leapfrog, Leapfrog, Snake, Snake	61	Teams of 2	Experienced	Any flat surface	Most	
19v	Leaping Circle Relay	39	Teams of 5-8	All	Any flat surface	Most	
100v	Long and Narrow	175	2 teams of 2	Expert	Volleyball court		
96v	Long-Ball Volleyball Relay	167	Teams of 4 or more	Expert	Volleyball court		
45	Long Cross and Drop	78	Pairs	Experienced	Badminton court		
10v	Long Dogs	27	Teams of 5-10	All	Any flat surface	Most	
52v	Long Game	91	Pairs	Expert	Badminton court		
10v	Loose Dog	27	Teams of 5-10	All	Any flat surface	Most	
42v	Low-Bird Juggle	72	1	Experienced	Any flat surface		
94v	Mass-Ball Shower Volleyball	163	2 teams of 6 or more	Experienced	Volleyball court		
33v	Mass Over, Under, and Around	57	Teams of 3	All	Any flat surface	Most	
65v	Mass Star Pass	112	Groups of 5, 7, 9, etc.	All	Any flat surface		
36v	Multishuffle Swamp Pass	60	Groups of 4-8	All	Any flat, smooth surface	Most	

Game number	Game	Page number	Number of players	Experience	Playing area	Sport	Cool-Down
90v	Multisport 2-4 Keep-Away	155	2 teams of 3-4	Experienced	Any flat surface		
82v	Multisport Crazy Eights	144	Any number	All	Any flat surface		
4v	Multisport Follow the Leader	19	Any number	All	A gymnasium floor with lines	Most	
89v	Multisport Grid Pass	153	Groups of 4	Experienced	Any flat surface	Most	
71v	Multisport Hot Ball or Puck	122	Groups of 7-15	All	Any flat surface		
55v	Multisport Jog Toss	97	Groups of 5 or more	All	Any flat surface		
76v	Multisport Obstacle Course	132	Teams of 3	All	Any flat surface	Most	
85v	Multisport Split Triangle Run	147	Teams of 3	All	Any flat surface	Most	
70v	Multisport Take-a-Break Keep-Away	120	2 teams of 3-6	Experienced	Any flat surface		
71v	Name Calling Hot Football	122	Groups of 7-15	All	Any flat surface		
54	Narrow, Clear, Smash, Drop	94	Pairs	Expert	Badminton court		
46	Next-in-Line Badminton	80	6-10 per court	Experienced	Badminton court		
94v	No-Pass Shower Volleyball	163	2 teams of 6 or more	Experienced	Volleyball court		
76	Obstacle Course for Hockey	132	Teams of 3	All	Ice surface		
31	Octopus	54	Teams of 2	Experienced	Any flat surface	Most	

Game number	Game	Page number	Number of players	Experience	Playing area	Sport	Cool-Down
93v	One-Bounce Soccer Volleyball (Tennis)	159	2 teams of 4	Expert	Volleyball court or tennis court		
87	One-Goal Soccer	149	Teams of 2-8	All	Any flat surface		
100v	One-on-One	175	2 teams of 1	Expert	Volleyball court		
27	Over and Under	49	Teams of 5-10	All	Gymnasium or large room	Most	
33	Over, Under, Around	57	Teams of 3	All	Any flat surface	Most	
64	Pass Around	110	Groups of 2	All	Any flat surface to sit on		
83	Pit Ball Terror	145	2 teams of 3-5	All	Any flat surface		
53	Played by the Book	93	Pairs	Expert	Badminton court		
5	Popcorn	20	Any size group	All	Any flat surface	Most	
57	Pop-Up One Bounce	99	Teams of 2	Experienced	Any flat field		
69	Professional Bump	117	5-50	Experienced	A basketball court with several baskets marked with free-throw lines		
78	Puck Handle Score!	135	Groups of 5-10	Experienced	Ice surface		
77v	Puck Soccer	134	Teams of 3-5	Experienced	Ice surface		
11	Pursuit Tag	28	10 or more	All	Any flat surface	Most	
2	Quick Zoo	16	Any number	All	A gymnasium	Most	
35	Rat Race	59	Any number; odd number works best	All	Any flat surface	Most	
68v	Rebounding Doubles	116	3 teams of 2	Experienced	An area with a basketball hoop		

Game number	Game	Page number	Number of players	Experience	Playing area	Sport	Cool-Down
68	Rebounding Trios	115	3 teams of 3	Experienced	An area with a basketball hoop		
61	Relay, Relay	104	2 or more teams of 3-8	Experienced	Any long, flat field		
62	Right-Left Consecutive Bunt Pepper	105	Teams of 4	Experienced	Any flat field		
71v	Rotating Hot Football	122	Groups of 7-15	All	Any flat surface		
73v	Round the Corners Lateral	126	Groups of 3	All	Any flat surface		
73v	Round the Corners Multisport Passes	126	Groups of 3	All	Any flat surface	Most	
73	Round the Corners Snap	125	Groups of 3	All	Any flat surface		
6	Running the Rails	21	Groups of 5 or more	All	Any flat surface	Most	
96v	Running Volleyball Relay	167	Teams of 4 or more	Experienced	Volleyball court		
11v	Scooter Pursuit	29	10 or more	All	Any flat surface	Most	
97	Setting Threes	168	Groups of 3	Experienced	Volleyball court		
67	Shoot for the Stars	114	1 at a time	Experienced	Basketball hoop with a key		
52	Short and Long Game	91	Pairs	Expert	Badminton court		
95v	Short Balloon Volleyball	165	2 or 4	Experienced	Volleyball court		
56	Short Relay	98	Teams of 3	Experienced	Any flat surface		
100	Short Volleyball	174	2 teams of 2	Expert	Volleyball court		
94	Shower Volleyball	162	2 teams of 6 or more	Experienced	Volleyball court		
22v	Shuffle Dribble	43	Teams of 3	All	Any flat surface		
22	Shuffle Run	43	Teams of 3	All	Any flat surface	Most	
46v	Side Subs Badminton	80	2 teams of 4	Experienced	Badminton court		

Game number	Game	Page number	Number of players	Experience	Playing area	Sport	Cool-Down
32v	Slalom Skier	56	Teams of 3-13	All	Any flat surface	Most	[fan]
11v	Slippery Pursuit	29	10 or more	All	Any flat surface	Most	[fan]
32	Snakeskin	55	Teams of 3-13	All	Any flat surface	Most	[fan]
14v	Soccer Ball Safe	32	Groups of 5-15	All	Any flat surface	[soccer ball]	[fan]
98v	Soccer Frozen Tag	171	Groups of 6 or more	Experienced	Any flat surface	[soccer ball]	[fan]
93v	Soccer Tennis	159	2 teams of 2	Expert	Tennis court	[soccer ball]	[fan]
93	Soccer Volleyball	158	2 teams of 4	Expert	Volleyball court	[soccer ball]	[fan]
92	Soccer Wallball	157	2	Experienced	An area with a wall	[soccer ball]	[fan]
8v	Space Dribble	24	Any number	All	Any flat surface	[basketball, football, hockey puck, soccer ball]	[fan]
8v	Space Jog	24	Any number	All	Any flat surface	Most	[fan]
8	Space Walk	24	Any number	All	Any flat surface	Most	[fan]
70v	Specific Pass Take-a-Break Keep-Away	120	2 teams of 3-6	Experienced	Any flat surface	[basketball]	[fan]
62v	Speed Pepper	106	Teams of 4	Experienced	Any flat field	[bat and ball]	[fan]
85	Split Triangle Run	147	Teams of 3	All	Any flat surface	[soccer ball]	[fan]
64v	Standing Pass Around	110	Groups of 2	All	Any flat surface	[basketball]	
65	Star Pass	111	Groups of 5	All	Any flat surface	[basketball]	[fan]
67v	Sure Shot for the Stars	114	1 at a time	Experienced	Basketball hoop with a key	[basketball]	[fan]
7	Swamp Monster	22	Any number	All	Any flat surface	Most	[fan]
36	Swamp Pass	60	Groups of 4-8	All	Any flat, smooth surface	Most	[fan]

Game number	Game	Page number	Number of players	Experience	Playing area	Sport	Cool-Down
70	Take-a-Break Keep-Away	119	2 teams of 3-6	Experienced	Any flat surface		
27v	Team Over and Under	49	Teams of 5-10	All	Gymnasium or large room	Most	
39	Team Run	66	Groups of 5-25	All	Any flat surface	Most	
39v	Team Sit-Ups	66	Groups of 5-25	All	Any flat surface	Most	
48v	Team Upset	85	At least 6 per court	Experienced	Badminton court		
99v	Ten Pass	173	2 teams of 6	Expert	Volleyball court		
43	Thread the Button	74	Teams of 5-8	Experienced	Half a badminton court		
62v	Through-the-Infield Pepper	106	Teams of 4	Experienced	Any flat field		
84	Throw-In Ball	146	2 teams of 3-9	All	Any flat surface		
85v	Throw-In Split Triangle Run	147	Teams of 3	All	Any flat surface		
63	Throw to a Wall Relay	108	Teams of 3	All	Any flat surface with a wall		
86v	Triple Cone Ball	148	Groups of 3	All	Any flat surface		
63v	Triple Pass Wall Relay	109	Teams of 3	All	Any flat surface with a wall		
59	Two-a-Side Fantasy Baseball	101	2 teams of 2	Experienced	Any flat field		
101v	Two-Ball Continuous Pass	177	12 or more	Expert	Volleyball court		
42v	Two-Bird Rally	73	1	Experienced	Any flat surface		
43v	Two-Bird Thread the Button	75	Teams of 5-8	Experienced	Half a badminton court		
80	Two-Line Pass	138	Groups of 5-10	Experienced	Ice surface		
34v	Two-Tube Hole in One	58	2 teams of 2-8	All	Any flat surface	Most	
68v	Two Rebounding Doubles	116	2 teams of 2	Experienced	An area with a basketball hoop		

Game number	Game	Page number	Number of players	Experience	Playing area	Sport	Cool-Down
68v	Two Rebounding Trios	116	2 teams of 3	Experienced	An area with a basketball hoop	🏀	
75	Ultimate Football	129	2 teams of 4-12	Experienced	Any flat field	🏈	💺
75v	Ultimate Soccer (or Hockey or Lacrosse)	130	2 teams of 4-12	Experienced	Any flat field	🏒⚽	💺
40	Under Frog	67	2 groups of 4-10	All	Any flat surface	Most	💺
64v	Up-and-Down Pass Around	110	Groups of 2	All	Any flat surface	🏀	
48	Upset	84	At least 3 per court	Experienced	Badminton court	🏸	💺
96	Volleyball Relay	166	Teams of 4 or more	Experienced	Volleyball court	🏐	💺
42v	Walking Bird Juggle	72	1	Experienced	Any flat surface	🏸	💺
11v	Walking Pursuit	29	10 or more	All	Any flat surface	Most	
3v	Weaver	18	Teams of 4-8	Experienced	Open space	Most	💺
72v	Wild Clothespins	124	Any number	All	Any flat surface	🏈	💺
72	Wild Flags	124	Any number	All	Any flat surface	🏈	💺
24v	Wobbly Arch and Roll Relay	45	Teams of 5-15	All	Any flat surface	🏈	💺
1v	Zipper	15	Teams of 5-35	All	Any flat surface	Most	💺

PREFACE

The value of warm-ups and cool-downs is well documented. Their advantages to players include decreased risk of injury, increased range of motion at the joints, improved coordination, and improved muscle readiness. Warm-ups are entrenched in the teaching and coaching of those leading physical education classes, competitive sports, and recreational activities. Unfortunately, warm-ups often consist of only some boring lap running and a bit of stretching. Why start a practice or class with something boring when the warm-up experience can begin the activity in an invigorating and motivating way? A good warm-up gets players on task right from the beginning. Engaging the players in warm-up games can create a great start.

This book will make the players' involvement in physically active games safer and more fun. By providing plenty of well-explained games, this book helps each practice or game start by engaging the whole player. The same games, sometimes with slight modifications, can also serve as effective exercises to cool down players at the end of a practice or class.

A good warm-up game can help prepare players physically and mentally for the activity. The warm-up provides a bridge from previous activities into the new world of game playing and practicing. These games can encourage players to practice previously learned skills and strategies. Because the games often involve small teams, each player will have plenty of contact with the equipment in an activity that requires greater mental concentration than just going for a run.

The leader (teacher or coach) also benefits from warm-ups. The leader can observe the ability and character (strengths and weaknesses) of the players. Because the games often involve fewer people, individual players must take responsibility for their own contributions. The leader can observe how well students take that responsibility.

A good cool-down helps return players to a more normal level by allowing the players' heart rates and enthusiasm (fewer shrieks of delight) to decrease from what they were at the height of the activity. The cool-down also allows the body to work off some waste products gained during the activity and helps venous blood return.

Being a physical education teacher, coach, recreation leader, and active player of games during my entire life, I love the joy of playing games. It is out of this passion, and out of years of leading and participating in games, that this book finds its roots. When I finished one of my most recent books, *Co-Ed Recreational Games* (2002), I began thinking about how a book of games for warm-ups and cool-downs would also add joy to the lives of people. When I discovered that there was no such book, I went to work.

This book has three sections. The introduction highlights the theory behind warm-ups and cool-downs. The second and third areas are the meat of the book, providing 101 games (and over a 101 variations). Part I provides games we can play for a variety of activities as a general warm-up. Part II provides games we can play for specific sports. If you provide your players opportunities to modify the games and create their own, they will often come up with great new variations.

The presentation of each game is sequentially organized. The number of players per group, the experience required, the type of playing area to be used, and the recommended equipment are identified first. The book instructs the leader on how to set up the game and identifies the key objective. Building on this foundational understanding of the game, the book then explains how the game is played. To make each game safe, unique safety instructions for each game are identified to protect the players. Instructional tips that enhance the success of the game are also offered. Variations to the main game are provided, usually making the game more complex. Finally, the book evaluates the suitability of the game as a cool-down activity and provides modifications that can make the game more effective as a cool-down. In each chapter the games are listed from easiest to most difficult.

Because players will need a little time to learn the games, leaders may want to alternate among a couple of games and their variations over several classes or practices. Reusing the games best uses class and practice time for activity while still maintaining fun variety.

The Game Finder helps the reader locate games quickly. The alphabetical listing includes the game number to assist in finding the game. Games are also identified for specific sports. A creative leader understands that many games that apply to hockey can apply to lacrosse, or that games that apply to basketball can also apply to netball.

Enjoy the book. Appreciate the feeling that those you are leading are safely preparing themselves for more intense activity. Most of all, enjoy watching players begin their practices and physical education classes with physical vigor, mental intensity, and plenty of laughter. Let's play!

ACKNOWLEDGMENTS

I want to thank my Canadian Intramural Recreation Association of Ontario peers for their incredible contributions to kids. A big thanks to Andy, Carolyn, Donna, Les, Michelle H., Michelle W., Rodney, Tina, and Wig.

THEORY OF WARM-UPS, COOL-DOWNS, AND STRETCHING

Warming up bodies, cooling them down, and stretching them are a helpful part of the training regime for sport participation, whether in a physical education class, a recreational game, or a competitive athletic contest. This book is specifically written to help leaders and those they instruct add fun to warm-ups and cool-downs, thus increasing their effectiveness. But what does research say about warm-ups, cool-downs, and stretching? Knowing the research helps us lead and participate in safe activities that are more likely to enhance game experience.

One of the premises of this book is that warm-ups and cool-downs can be fun. Before turning to the research on warm-ups, cool-downs, and stretching, what does the literature say about fun? People find a sense of fun, joy, and enrichment as they involve themselves in game participation (26, 53, 89). Yet one of the first things leaders often do is have players run around the gym or field at the beginning of a class or practice. This running around is both good and bad. Running is good in that the body begins to warm up for more strenuous activity, but it can be harmful because it does not satisfy the fun, joy, and enrichment that attracted players to the experience in the first place. When players experience not fun but failure, they are more inclined to drop out of the activity (35). Although we cannot make people have fun, as leaders we should strive to create opportunities and a tone to instruction that include fun as a central component of the physical activity (49, 50, 65, 74, 94, 96, 101).

WARM-UPS

Although most people engage in some form of warm-up before beginning physical activity, the first issue concerns why we do warm-ups. The research demonstrates the importance of warming up and helps define how to do warm-ups effectively.

Why Warm Up?

The main reason for using warm-ups is to minimize risk of injury. Warm-ups also serve to enhance physiological and psychological preparedness for the activity.

The issue of using warm-ups to reduce injuries finds writers on opposite ends of a scale. Some school authorities legally require warm-ups in physical education classes to minimize the possibility of injury (54). On the other end, at least three researchers conclude that warm-ups "do not aid in the prevention of DOMS (delayed-onset muscle soreness) associated with heavy exhaustive exercise," but cautiously add that "more research is needed to determine if such conclusions are valid for other intensities of exercise, warm-ups, and/or stretching" (51). The prevailing wisdom, however, is that generalized muscle activity in a warm-up "is very important to increase muscle temperature that has shown to decrease MTU (muscle-tendon unit) stiffness, allow greater permanent elongation of muscles and tendons (93), and increase the maximum strain and stress the MTU can resist before injury" (63, 75, 92).

When the body becomes more active during a warm-up, the player's pulse rises, enhancing the aerobic capacity of the player. This higher pulse and general body warming increase the total oxygen in the bloodstream, blunt blood lactate response, increase vasodilation of blood vessels, and increase the ability of hemoglobin in red blood cells to release oxygen (15, 18, 21, 33, 34, 36, 42, 45, 48, 76, 78, 87, 98). In another study, some players acted as a control group and did not warm up before performing a skill, while other players performed different warm-ups. All of the players who did a warm-up scored significantly higher than the control group that used no warm-up. These results led one researcher to conclude that at least any active warm-up is better than no warm-up (19). Overall, a body that is warmed up through preliminary activity is better able to respond physiologically to activity than a body that is not warmed up.

Our bodies go through daily cycles. One of those cycles involves changes in core body temperature. Our body temperature is at its lowest at 4:00 A.M. and rises until it peaks at approximately 6:00 P.M. (6, 9, 12, 85). In terms of warm-ups, this means that the activity level needs to be higher or longer in the morning to compensate for lower body temperature. In a specific study done on swimming, it was determined that "swim performance can be maintained with a 66% reduction in warm-up volume" in an afternoon swim compared with a morning swim (7).

A warmed body also improves coordination because nerve impulse transmission is more rapid at higher temperatures (17). One study found that baseball players and gymnasts who engaged in a warm-up on a bicycle ergometer following a period of rest did not experience the performance decrement suffered by a control group who did not use a warm-up (51). Other studies also support the importance of a warm-up on the central nervous system (4, 18, 58, 65, 71, 102). Warmer muscles facilitate faster and stronger muscle contractions and greater muscle relaxation time (14, 17, 27, 45). Warm-ups prepare players neurologically and psychologically for the activity.

To add interest through greater variety in warm-ups, to use time efficiently, and to increase learning opportunities, warm-ups can build effectively on previously learned skills or incorporate new skills by including sport-specific activities (31, 54, 69). Pitching a baseball before a game (38), throwing a football before a game, doing several practice golf swings before a round, or lifting some lighter weights before building up to higher intensity helps players better prepare for competition (101). Incorporating activity-specific warm-ups can also prevent player boredom and enhance performance (101). In an experiment using tennis skills, tennis players practiced various strokes, entered a rest period, performed one of a variety of warm-ups, and then underwent testing. The warm-ups consisted of running in place, imagery, air dribbling, and practice swings. The control group that did not warm up had the largest decrement in skills, and those who used imagery had the next largest decline. Those who ran in place showed significant improvement, but air dribbling and practice swings contributed the most to skill performance. The study concluded by suggesting that "an effective warm-up for applied open skills should include the physical performance of activities that direct the player's attention to relevant aspects of the task" (102). In another study measuring for vertical jump, "the highest vertical jump scores were obtained with a specific warm-up using the weighted jumping warm-up procedure." This result led the researchers to conclude that "when constructing a warm-up, the concepts of specificity and overload should play a large role" (19). Part of the explanation may be that warming up using movements similar to the intended activity prepares the body neurologically for the impending activity (22, 103). Warm-ups can serve as integral lead-in activities. Practicing skills during a warm-up uses the warm-up to full advantage; the book takes that approach.

Summing up, an effective warm-up

➤ reduces the risk of injury,
➤ gradually increases heart rate and blood circulation,
➤ increases body temperature,
➤ improves efficiency of muscular actions,
➤ improves transmission of nerve impulses,
➤ permits freer movements in the joints,
➤ prepares the joints and associated muscles to function through their full range of motion, and
➤ aids psychological preparation for the activity to follow (49).

How to Warm Up

The length of a warm-up depends on several factors:

➤ The intensity of the activity to follow (that is, how energetic it is going to be)
➤ The duration of the activity to follow (that is, how long it is going to last)
➤ The current activity or fitness levels of the players
➤ Environmental factors such as room and air temperature (49)

Although experienced athletes spend considerable time warming up—college baseball pitchers warm up on average for 40 minutes (38)—it is felt that "too little time is often spent on warm-up activities in the school or recreation class" (54). The common excuse is that if a teacher had, for example, a 30-minute class and allowed 5 minutes for students to get to class and get ready, 5 minutes for warm-up, 5 minutes for cool-down, and 5 minutes for stretching, she would be left with 10 minutes of instructional and activity time. But if the warm-up and cool-down activities lead into and reinforce the lesson's activities, they would not impede instruction but improve it. Because the instructional activity is brief, the warm-up and cool-down can also be brief. In general, it is recommended that players perform 5 to 10 minutes of low-intensity aerobic exercise to elevate the body temperature (24, 65). The warm-up should usually not exceed 10 to 15 minutes (101).

To gain maximum benefits from the warm-up, it should immediately precede the activity. For example, one study determined that there was an "increase in spine stiffness as a result of a prolonged bench rest after a warm-up" (46). This finding means that athletes who start a game on the bench need to find ways for remaining warm and sitting less (20, 41, 64, 67) so that when they are called on they can perform effectively and not face high risk of back injury. Likewise, when demonstration of an activity requires players to be inactive for a considerable time (especially if they are sitting), instructors should give the bulk of those instructions before a warm-up. They can then provide a brief review before players practice the new activity. Too often classes and practices begin with a warm-up that is followed by a rest period during which the leader gives instructions. Players then execute the activity. This sequence is not helpful. Having a rest period following a warm-up reduces the effectiveness of the warm-up (5, 102). Players should warm up and then go directly into the activity!

Various researchers have recommended different intensities. One author felt that warm-ups should increase the heart rate by 10 to 30 beats per minute above the resting rate (65). Other studies have shown improvements from warm-ups at 50% of maximum heart rate (4, 5) or at 60% of $\dot{V}O_2$ maximum (57). But researchers have also found that a warm-up at excessive intensity may cause a decrease in maximal performance (29). As a general guideline the warm-up should increase the heart rate to approximately 55% of maximum heart rate. This heart rate can be quickly calculated by subtracting a person's age from 220 and multiplying by .55. For example, a 20-year-old has a maximum heart rate of 200 (220 − 20) and should be warming up at approximately 110 beats per minute (200 × .55).

Ten-year-old children should be around 115 beats per minute by the end of the warm-up (49).

Summing up the research, warm-ups are an important part of preparing for strenuous activity. An adequate warm-up prepares the player both physically and psychologically for activity, enhances performance, and likely reduces risk of injury. General warm-ups are important, but activity-specific warm-ups are more effective for preparing the player for successfully and safely engaging in the activity. The more sport specific the warm-up, the more focused the entire class or practice will be.

COOL-DOWNS

Cool-downs are helpful following strenuous activity. Again, the inquisitive reader will want to know why we should do cool-downs and how we should do them. The research demonstrates the importance of performing cool-downs and helps define how to do them effectively.

Why Cool Down?

Active players need to overcome muscle fatigue quickly after exercise to experience full recovery. Recovery has been defined as "the ability of an individual to return to or toward the rested state" (13). One of the keys to recovery, particularly following a demanding workout, is an active cooling-down period (79). This time allows the body temperature to return to normal. The cool-down should be active enough to wash away muscle metabolism by-products such as lactic acid. Lactate concentration is an important indicator of recovery (8, 70). An active cool-down reduces any tendency toward postexercise fainting and dizziness and limits the pooling of blood in lower extremities from a sudden stop in exercise (18).

Reducing injury or fatigue promotes future involvement in exercise and physical activity. Aching muscles are unhappy reminders of previous activity. People tend to remember their most recent exertion; therefore, in an exercise class a cool-down may have a beneficial psychological effect because the session ends on a gentler note. The cool-down can also be a fun time to bring players' energy levels down. A dance instructor noted that "the cool-down is the perfect time for dancers to let their hair down and enjoy a laugh by experimenting with funky moves" (28). One can also use mind- or body-inspired moves adapted from martial-arts movements (97).

Summing up, an effective cool-down

➤ decreases the heart rate and blood circulation gradually;

➤ aids venous return (by maintaining contraction of the leg muscles to help prevent blood from pooling in the legs and to assist the return of blood to the heart);

➤ assists in the removal of waste products (particularly lactic acid, which may have built up as a by-product of vigorous anaerobic work such as sprinting or jumping), allowing a quicker and more comfortable recovery from exercise;

➤ helps minimize postexercise muscle stiffness and soreness; and

➤ returns the body safely and effectively to a preexercise condition (49).

How to Cool Down

To cool down, players should engage in sport-specific movements at about half intensity. Players can then do quarter-speed jogging (which may take place when returning from a playing field to the locker rooms) and finally perform some stretching (70, 86). The cool-down should last for 3 to 5 minutes, or longer if the intensity of the activity was very high (18, 24, 49).

STRETCHING

The primary purpose of stretching is to reduce injury and enhance performance through increased flexibility of the muscles and tendons. Flexibility is defined as the "intrinsic property of the body tissues which determines the range of motion achievable without injury at a joint or group of joints" (52). Many consider stretching an important part of a warm-up (101) and crucial to improving flexibility for life. Although research supports the use of stretching to serve the latter purpose, the use of stretching in warm-ups finds little support in research (23, 43, 60, 82, 92), a surprising result considering its popular use in that role. Research findings do encourage stretching following activity (62).

The three commonly used types of stretching are static, ballistic, and proprioceptive neuromuscular facilitation (PNF). Static stretching involves slowly moving a muscle group to a stretched position and holding it for 15 to 30 seconds. Ballistic stretching involves quick, momentum-assisted stretches created by swinging a body segment.

PNF stretching involves contraction of muscles against a trained assistant's resistance, followed by relaxation and an assistant's force. Although the last type of exercise is perhaps the most effective at increasing flexibility, it takes more time than other stretching techniques and requires skilled assistants (2, 37, 66, 84, 91, 99). Most exercise and physiology textbooks recommend avoiding ballistic stretching because injury may result from the athlete's efforts to lengthen the muscle while the myotatic reflex is contracting (32, 39, 80, 82, 88).

One of the reasons not to stretch during warm-ups is that doing so reduces performance. Research found that strength decreases following the use of any of the three stretching types (10, 30, 40, 47, 59, 72, 90). Therefore, researchers recommend that "intense stretching of muscles should not be undertaken just before any event in which success is related to maximal strength output" (73). In particular, stretching should be minimized before such activities as sprinting and jumping (23), power lifting, or rock climbing (62), in which performance measures decreased by 3 to 8% after stretching (25, 59, 63, 72, 90). The only exceptions appear to be sports requiring flexibility beyond normal range of motion such as gymnastics or dance (62).

Another reason not to stretch in warm-ups is to reduce risk of injury. Cooler muscles and tendons are stiffer and more easily damaged than warm muscles are; therefore, it is safer to stretch following an activity (during the cool-down) than before the activity (during the warm-up) (18, 75, 92, 93). Stretching should thus be performed not during warm-ups but at the end of a class, practice, or competition as a means to minimize injury, to avoid compromising performance, and to enhance flexibility for life (23, 62, 65, 66).

The prevailing wisdom is that players should hold each stretch approximately 15 to 30 seconds (11, 16, 63, 65, 81). Although this may seem to be a long time, these 15- to 30-second periods can be fun and productive. Players can count aloud to 45 (players usually count two numbers each second so counting to 45 should work out well for time). For added variation each student can take a turn counting one number. For more fun, players can count in different languages or count backward. An instructor can use the time during the stretches as a teaching moment to ask players questions related to the material or activities covered during the session. These stretching periods also give the leader an opportunity to discuss what is planned for the next class or practice.

The intensity of the stretch should be "just before discomfort" (61). One of the other keys to the development of flexibility is increasing the strength of the opposite muscle (56, 68, 99). For example, to increase flexibility of the hamstrings, players should increase the strength of the quadriceps. Sufficient research has not been done on the frequency of stretching and long-term flexibility (95). Prevailing wisdom, however, recommends stretching at least 3 days a week, preferably daily or after all workouts (61). Table 1 provides a summary of stretching recommendations supported by current research.

Several teaching points and phrases are useful in teaching stretches:

> Ease into the stretch slowly.
> Hold the stretch still; do not bounce.
> Feel mild tension in the middle of the stretched muscle.
> If you feel any pain or the muscle starts shaking, ease off the stretch immediately.
> Relax all other parts of your body, particularly your head, shoulders, and back.

TABLE 1	Stretching Recommendations Supported by Current Research
Frequency	Stretching should be performed at least three times per week, preferably daily or after all workouts.
Intensity	The appropriate intensity is to stretch slowly and hold the elongated muscle-tendon units at low force levels. Players should use minimal rate of stretch and forces.
Time	Stretching for flexibility should be performed during the cool-down phase of the workout. Players should perform up to four or five stretches for each muscle group, holding each for 15 to 30 seconds.
Type	The preferred mode of stretching involves static or PNF stretching techniques.

Reprinted with permission from *The Journal of Physical Education, Recreation & Dance*, March 1998, p. 39. *JOPERD* is a publication of the American Alliance for Health, Physical Education, Recreation and Dance, 1900 Association Dr., Reston, VA 20191.

➤ Don't fight against the muscle; try to relax.
➤ If comfortable and the muscle feels relaxed, try increasing the stretch gently and holding the new position still.
➤ Gently ease out of the stretch (49).

The focus of this book is on warm-ups and cool-downs. The activities suggested here will help players warm up and cool down. Stretching deserves a book of its own. I recommend Michael Alter's *Science of Flexibility* (2004), available through Human Kinetics. Human Kinetics has also produced several valuable posters and videos, including *Teaching Flexibility Video* (1997), *Flexibility for Sport and Fitness Video* (1997), *Testing Your Flexibility Poster* (1997), and *Stretching/ Flexibility Poster Set* (1997).

SUMMING UP

Low-intensity warm-ups should immediately precede physical activity. Ideally, the warm-up will pertain to the activity. For low-level recreational activity the warm-up can be relatively brief; for high-intensity athletic activity the warm-up should be longer. Except for some basic limbering up, no stretching should occur before the activity. For performance and safety the body needs to be warmed before engaging in strenuous activity. Following the activity, players should engage in a brief period of activity-related cooling down and some stretches. The stretching is intended for long-term flexibility. Like the warm-up, if the activity is not intense the cool-down can be simple and less intense; if the activity is extremely intense the cool-down should be longer. The warm-ups, cool-downs, and stretching will benefit players by improving their performance, minimizing injury, and speeding recovery. Fun warm-ups and cool-downs are great ways to begin and conclude classes, practices, and games.

PART I

GENERAL WARM-UP AND COOL-DOWN GAMES

CHAPTER 1

QUICK MOVEMENT GAMES

1. High Fives

Number of players	Experience	Playing area
Teams of 5-35	All	Any flat surface

Recommended Equipment
None.

Setup
Players are in two lines facing each other in a staggered formation. Players are two to four paces apart.

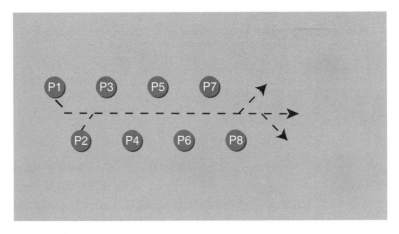

Key Objective
For players to warm up by high-fiving each other for a set time or distance.

How to Play
Player 1 (P1) runs between the two rows of players, high-fiving each player. When P1 reaches the end of the rows, she stands two to four paces past P7. When P1 passes P2, P2 follows P1, and when P2 reaches the end of the rows, he stands two to four paces past P8. P3 follows P2, P4 follows P3, and so on. The team can high-five for 1 or 2 minutes or for a set distance (once around the soccer field).

Safety Considerations
To avoid running into one another, players should not follow too closely behind each other.

Instructional Tips

➤ This game is a fun, quickly organized activity.

➤ If many players are involved have them stand closer together. With fewer players have them stand further apart.

➤ With an even number of players the players stay on the same side of the line. With an odd number of players the players change sides each time they do their runs.

Variation

Zipper: Players form two lines facing each other, as in High Fives, and stretch both hands in front of themselves so that they almost touch the player opposite them. When a player runs between the lines the other players lift their arms just before the runner would touch them. Besides providing a warm-up this game builds trust.

Cool-Down

This game also works well as a cool-down. Players should go at half speed or do a round or two of Zipper.

2. Quick Zoo

Number of players	Experience	Playing area
Any number	All	A gymnasium

Recommended Equipment
Pictures of various animals.

Setup
Post various pictures of animals around the gym walls.

Key Objective
To warm up through movement and have slower exercise breaks to mimic animals.

How to Play
Players are distributed along the edge of the gym. At the signal to begin, they all begin to jog (or use another prescribed movement) until a signal is given to run. When the signal is given to stop, each student points to the animal picture closest to him and begins to move around the gym mimicking the movements of that animal. At the next signal to go, the players resume a regular run. At the signal to stop, players stop, point to the animal picture closest to them, and begin to move around the gym mimicking the movements of that animal.

Cool-Down
The game works well as a cool-down.

3. Front of the Class

Number of players	Experience	Playing area
Teams of 4-8	Experienced	Open space

Recommended Equipment
Cones.

Setup
Define an area with four cones or use an existing court (volleyball court, outdoor soccer goal crease) and position players standing behind each other in a single file line.

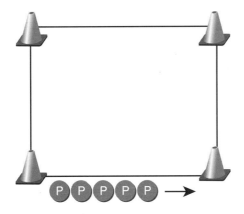

Key Objective
Players jog past each other, on the team's right when moving counterclockwise, to the front of the line until all players are back in their original positions.

How to Play
The group starts a slow jog around the court. The player in the back of the line runs on the outside of the group to the front of the line. When that player makes it to the front, the player who is now the last player runs to the front of the line. They continue until all are back in their original positions.

Safety Considerations
Players should exercise caution when taking the corners.

Instructional Tips

The group should not run so quickly that the back player cannot make it to the front of the line, nor should they run so slowly that the players gain no exercise benefits.

Variations

➤ **Front of the Sport Dribble Class:** Players run as they do in Front of the Class except that they dribble a ball (basketball, soccer ball) or hockey puck.

➤ **Base Runners:** Players run as they do in Front of the Class except that they run around the bases of a baseball diamond.

➤ **Weaver:** Players run as they do in Front of the Class or Front of the Sport Dribble Class except that the player in the back does not run past teammates on the side of the line but weaves in and out through the moving line.

Cool-Down

Players do the same activity, but the player in the back runs across the inside of the court to the front of the line.

4. Follow the Leader

Number of players	Experience	Playing area
Any size group	All	A gymnasium floor with lines

Recommended Equipment
None.

Setup
Students line up single file behind a leader.

Key Objective
For all players to follow the player in front of them and repeat the same movements.

How to Play
All players follow the leader down lines in the gym. The leader uses different movements to go down the line (hopping, long steps, going backward, crab walk, sideways, cartwheels, and so on). At a cue given by the instructor, the leader goes to the back of the line and a new leader leads the team.

Safety Considerations
Warn students not to do dangerous movements (hopping over chairs, running along benches).

Instructional Tips
Some fun and lively music will enhance this activity. Players enjoy having the opportunity to lead.

Variation
Multisport Follow the Leader: Provide each player with a piece of equipment, for example, a basketball. The leader dribbles with the right hand, the next leader dribbles with the left hand, the next leader dribbles backward, and the next leader picks another way of dribbling. Change leaders every 15 to 30 seconds.

Cool-Down
This game works well as a cool-down (use slower music).

5. Popcorn

Number of players	Experience	Playing area
Any size group	All	Any flat surface

Recommended Equipment
Storage container and 20 to 30 beanbags.

Setup
Players spread themselves around the playing area. The container with the beanbags and one player designated as the popcorn maker are at the center of the playing area.

Key Objective
For the players to keep the container full of popcorn while the popcorn maker tries to empty the popcorn from the container one beanbag at a time.

How to Play
At the leader's signal to start, the popcorn maker tries to throw all the popcorn out, one at a time, in an effort to empty the container. The rest of the players try to get the beanbags and toss them back into the container, making sure that the container always has some popcorn in it. The popcorn maker cannot intentionally block players from returning the popcorn into the container. If the popcorn maker wins or becomes too tired, assign a new popcorn maker.

Safety Considerations
Players near the popcorn maker need to avoid being hit by the popcorn maker or the popcorn being thrown out. A safer method is to have one or several designated players place the popcorn back into the container instead of all players.

Instructional Tips
This game can also be an entertaining way to clean up after a sport session. To get the volleyballs, basketballs, or soccer balls back into a bin, the teacher may want to be the popcorn maker and deliberately lose the game so that the players gather up all the equipment.

Cool-Down
Try this game in slow motion for a cool-down.

6. Running the Rails

Number of players	Experience	Playing area
Groups of 5 or more	All	Any flat surface

Recommended Equipment
None.

Setup
Players lie in a row facedown beside each other (like railway ties on a railway), approximately half a step apart.

Key Objective
To measure how quickly a team can safely run the distance of a gym or field by running over each other.

How to Play
The first player lying in the line stands up and runs over the top of his teammates and lies down beside the last player in the line. Once the first player has gone over the second player, the second player stands up and runs over her teammates and lies down beside the last player in the line (who is the first player who ran). Players continue until they reach the established distance.

Safety Considerations
➤ Players should not run too fast and risk falling on each other.
➤ If the surface is slippery, runners may fall when running.

Variation
Double Track: This variation is the same as Running the Rails except that two teams compete against each other. Be sure that all players have experience with Running the Rails before making this a competitive event.

Cool-Down
This activity is too vigorous to use as a cool-down.

7. Swamp Monster

Number of players	Experience	Playing area
Any number	All	Any flat surface

Recommended Equipment
Ten to 15 gymnastics mats and some fun and lively music (CD player or tape player).

Setup
Spread mats out on the floor far enough apart that players can pass between them. Players distribute themselves around the floor not touching a mat.

Key Objective
For players to get on a mat when the music stops.

How to Play
Play the music. Tell players to use a specific locomotor pattern (skipping, hopping, galloping, and so forth) to move around the mats. If they make contact with a mat, the swamp monster gets them. To free themselves and rejoin the game, they have to perform 10 jumping jacks on the mat. When the music stops, players must find a mat by themselves and perform a balance. If no mats are left (or if they lose their balance), they have to run a lap around the outside of the playing area while everyone else gets a break. If two players end up on one mat at the same time, they both have to run a lap!

Safety Considerations
Players need to be aware of each other so that they do not bump into each other.

Instructional Tips
- ➤ Kids love this great gymnastics warm-up.
- ➤ Add to the fun occasionally by folding up the mats and placing them toward the outside so that the students have to leap over them as they do their laps.

Variation
Eliminating Swamp Monsters: Combine Swamp Monster and musical chairs by eliminating a mat after each turn.

Cool-Down

This game can work well as a cool-down if players walk. Eliminating Swamp Monsters works well at the end of a session because the players clean up all the mats during the game.

8. Space Walk

Number of players	Experience	Playing area
Any number	All	Any flat surface

Recommended Equipment

None.

Setup

Players distribute themselves in a defined area (gym, field, playing court).

Key Objective

For players to keep two paces between themselves and everyone else while continuously moving.

How to Play

At the leader's signal to start, all players begin to walk inside the defined area and try to keep two paces between themselves and any other player. Whenever two players get closer than two paces, both have 1 point scored against them. Points are scored on the honor system and the leader's observations. The leader must call out who got too close. The player who scores the fewest points wins.

Instructional Tips

This activity teaches players about finding open spaces.

Variations

- ➤ **Space Jog:** This game is the same as Space Walk except that players jog.
- ➤ **Space Dribble:** This variation is the same as Space Walk except that players dribble a ball or puck (basketball, soccer, hockey, or football if you want to have a really wacky time).

Cool-Down

This activity works well as a cool-down if players walk.

CHAPTER 2

TAG

9. Continuous Scooter Tag

Number of players	Experience	Playing area
Any number	All	Any flat surface

Recommended Equipment
One scooter per player; scooters of at least two different colors.

Setup
All players are seated on a scooter.

Key Objective
To avoid becoming an it.

How to Play
Designate a certain color of scooters to be it. Ideally, you have an equal number of scooters in two different colors; otherwise, pick the color you have most of. Let's say the colors are red and yellow, and we designate yellow as the it. On the leader's signal to go, the players move around the playing area. The players on yellow scooters try to tag players on red scooters. When a player from a yellow scooter tags a player on a red scooter, they switch scooters and the new player on the yellow scooter becomes an it. The new it cannot tag the player who just tagged him. Play continues for a specified time.

Safety Considerations
Players should watch that their fingers do not become caught under the scooter wheels.

Variation
Continuous Scooter Dribble Tag: This variation is like Continuous Scooter Tag except that all players have a ball that they must bounce when moving.

Cool-Down
This activity is too vigorous for a cool-down.

10. Dog's Tail

Number of players	Experience	Playing area
Teams of 5-10	All	Any flat surface

Recommended Equipment
None.

Setup
Teams line up with each player holding on to the waist of the player in front of her.

Key Objective
For the head of the dog (player in the front of the line) to tag the dog's tail (the player at the end of the line).

How to Play
The player in front tries to tag the back player. If the front player is successful the head player becomes the dog's tail.

Safety Considerations
If the dog turns too quickly the dog's tail will fly off.

Variations
➤ **Loose Dog:** One player (loose dog) is not attached to the dog (line of players).The loose dog tries to tag the dog's tail (player at the back of the line). When the loose dog is successful, she becomes the dog's tail and the dog's head (first player in line) becomes the next loose dog.

➤ **Long Dogs:** Several lines of players form dogs. The head of each dog (first player) tries to tag the tail of another dog (last player in line). When a dog's tail is tagged, it is added to the end of the tagging dog. The goal is to become the longest dog during a set time limit.

Cool-Down
This game is a fun and effective cool-down.

11. Pursuit Tag

Number of players	Experience	Playing area
10 or more	All	Any flat surface

Recommended Equipment
Twelve cones.

Setup

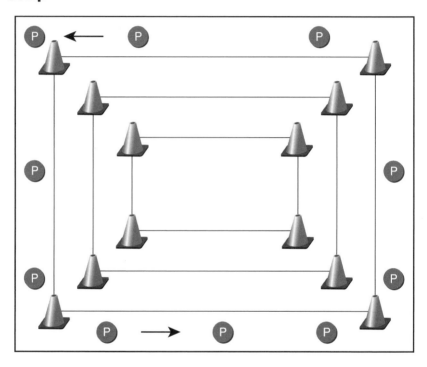

Key Objective
To avoid being tagged from behind.

How to Play
Everyone runs outside the outside cones. When players are tagged from behind they run inside the lane inside the outside cones. When players are tagged in the middle lane they move to the inside lane. When players are tagged in the inside lane they move to the outside lane. After a set time limit (2 to 3 minutes) the player who was tagged the fewest times is the winner.

Safety Considerations

Make sure corners are safe distances from the walls in case players lose their balance and fall.

Instructional Tips

The instructor may need to stress individual honesty when asking the players to count the number of times they have been tagged.

Variations

➤ **Walking Pursuit:** In this variation players must always have one foot on the ground.

➤ **Slippery Pursuit:** Instead of running and walking, players have to stand on two small pieces of carpet (towels) and shuffle as quickly as possible.

➤ **Scooter Pursuit:** This game is played in pairs with one partner pushing the other partner, who is seated on two scooters. The player on the scooters uses a pool noodle to tag the player in front.

Cool-Down

Except for Slippery Pursuit, this game is a little too vigorous to serve as a cool-down.

12. Continuous British Bulldog

Number of players	Experience	Playing area
Any number	All	Any flat surface

Recommended Equipment
None.

Setup
Establish a playing area with sidelines and two end lines. For groups of less than 10 players the court might be the size of a volleyball court; for groups of more than 75 the court might be the size of half a soccer field. All players stand at one of the end lines. Select one or several its, who stand in the middle of the court.

Key Objective
To avoid becoming an it.

How to Play
The its yell, "British Bulldog!" At that command all players must attempt to cross from one end line to the other, within the sidelines, without being tagged by an it. Players tagged by an it become new its. Any it who tags another player joins the group behind the end line. The game continues for about 5 minutes.

Safety Considerations
No rough play is permitted.

Variation
Continuous Basketball British Bulldog: Each player has a basketball. The players who are moving from one end line to the other and the its who are trying to tag them must all continuously dribble a basketball. If a player loses his basketball he becomes a new it. If an it loses his basketball he cannot tag anyone until he retrieves his ball.

Cool-Down
Assign about a third of the players to be its. Have them begin at one end line and the other players begin at the opposite end line.

13. Flusher

Number of players	Experience	Playing area
Any number	All	Any flat surface

Recommended Equipment

None.

Setup

Define a playing area. For 20 players half a volleyball court is about right.

Key Objective

For the it to tag all the other players (for added fun the it must tag the players with a toilet brush) without the players being flushed.

How to Play

Players distribute themselves around the court, and one player is designated as the it. When the it tags a player, that player must kneel on one knee and hold up an arm at a 90-degree angle. The down players can be freed when other players "flush the toilet" by pushing the kneeling player's hand down.

Safety Considerations

Players need to keep their heads up so that they do not run into each other.

Instructional Tips

Players may not complete this novel game, so a time limit may need to be established or more its designated.

Cool-Down

This game works well as a cool-down if the court size is enlarged to reduce the amount of running (with a larger area, more players are farther away from the it and can walk and rest more).

14. Ball Safe

Number of players	Experience	Playing area
Groups of 5-15	All	Any flat surface

Recommended Equipment
Two balls per group.

Setup
All players stand inside a specified area (half a basketball court). Two players hold balls. One player is assigned to be it.

Key Objective
To avoid being tagged by the it.

How to Play
This game is played like any tag game except that a player holding a ball is safe. Players attempt to prevent the not-its from being tagged by tossing them a ball so that they are safe.

Safety Considerations
Use soft foam balls so that players are not hurt if the ball hits them when they are not expecting it.

Instructional Tips
Players must learn to anticipate where the it is going and communicate with each other about passing the ball.

Variation
Soccer Ball Safe: This variation is the same as Ball Safe except that players kick the balls to each other. Players who hold a ball under one of their feet are safe and cannot be tagged.

Cool-Down
The game works well as a cool-down if more balls are used.

15. Knee Tag

Number of players	Experience	Playing area
Any number of pairs	All	Any flat surface

Recommended Equipment
None.

Setup
Players stand facing a partner approximately one or two paces apart.

Key Objective
For the players to touch their opponent's knees more times than their own knees are touched.

How to Play
At the leader's signal to begin, players attempt to use their hands to touch their partner's knees as often as possible while preventing their partner from touching their knees. At the end of 30 seconds the game ends and winners are determined (if tied, the player who first reached the point total wins). Players find a new partner. Winners find partners from among those who won, and the others find partners from among those who lost.

Safety Considerations
Players must be careful not to bump heads when moving to touch their partner's knees.

Instructional Tips
The activity teaches balanced positioning.

Cool-Down
The game is too vigorous to use as a cool-down.

16. Island Tag

Number of players	Experience	Playing area
Groups of 10 or more	All	Any flat surface

Recommended Equipment
Rope 30 yards or meters long for 10 players; a longer rope if playing with more players.

Setup
Place the rope in a long, narrow shape on the ground. The chosen shape can vary. All players must stand inside the roped area. Players should be tightly bunched together. If there is too much room, make the area smaller.

Key Objective
For players to avoid being tagged by the it.

How to Play
Each player partners up with another player. One of the players is designated as the it (a quick game of paper-scissor-rock can determine the first it). On the leader's signal to go, the it spins around twice on one spot to give her partner an opportunity to get away. The its then chase their partners. When a partner is tagged the partner becomes the new it, spins around twice on one spot, and gives chase. If a player goes off the island (outside the roped area), she is it. Play continues until sufficient time passes as long as players are still enjoying the game.

Safety Considerations
Do not allow players to run. Running will be difficult anyway because the game is played in tight quarters.

Variation
Blinders Island Tag: This variation is like Island Tag with two exceptions. First, players place one hand beside one of their eyes as a sort of blinder. Second, players place one hand straight in front of them to prevent themselves from inadvertently bumping into the other players. Players use their blinders and straight arms throughout the entire game.

Cool-Down
This game works great as a cool-down, especially if the roped area is very small so that players cannot move quickly.

17. Everyone It Frozen Tag

Number of players	Experience	Playing area
Any number	All	Any flat surface

Recommended Equipment
None.

Setup
Players stand in random positions throughout a designated area (for example, 7 players could play inside a badminton court; 15 players could play inside half a volleyball court).

Key Objective
To avoid being frozen.

How to Play
Everyone is it. If a player is tagged by another it, both of the tagged player's feet are frozen to the ground (the tagged player cannot move either foot). If a frozen player tags one of the its, the it becomes a frozen player and the frozen player thaws out and becomes an it again. Play continues until one it remains or for a specified time.

Instructional Tips
Players will quickly realize that they need to be aware of their spatial relationship with all other players.

Cool-Down
This activity can be a fun cool-down.

18. Balance Tag

Number of players	Experience	Playing area
Any number	All	Any flat surface

Recommended Equipment
One beanbag per player and one pool noodle per it.

Setup
Players take positions within a designated area, each with a beanbag on his head. The it has a pool noodle.

Key Objective
For the it to tag another player and for players to avoid losing their beanbags.

How to Play
At a signal to start, the it tries to tag another player on the torso with the pool noodle. If any player's beanbag falls off, he automatically becomes the it. (If it is too difficult for players to keep the beanbags on their heads, they can stop and place them on their heads again before moving. But if a player is tagged without a beanbag on his head, he is it). If a player is tagged with the pool noodle, he becomes the next it.

Instructional Tips
Adding more its creates a more active game.

Variations
➤ **Dribble Balance Tag:** This variation is the same as Balance Tag except that players must also dribble a basketball, soccer ball, or hockey puck.
➤ **Balance Any Tag:** Use Balance Tag for any tag game.

Cool-Down
With one or a few its, this game works well as a cool-down.

CHAPTER 3

RELAYS

19. Circle Relay

Number of players	Experience	Playing area
Teams of 5-8	All	Any flat surface

Recommended Equipment
None.

Setup
Players stand equal distance apart in a circle formation with a diameter of at least eight paces.

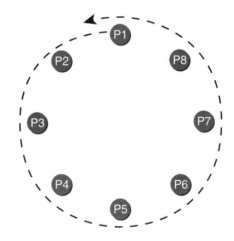

Key Objective
To complete the relay as quickly as possible.

How to Play
Player 1 (P1) runs completely around the outside of the circle and then tags P2. P1 takes P2's spot in the circle, and P2 runs around and tags P3. When all players in the circle complete their run the game is over. Time the players to see how quickly they can do it, or have them compete against other circles to see which team finishes first.

Safety Considerations
Make sure the floor is free of debris so that players do not slip when running around the outside of the circle.

Variations

➤ **Dribble Circle Relay:** This variation is the same as Circle Relay except that the player running around the circle dribbles a ball (basketball, soccer ball, hockey ball, or hockey puck) and gives it to the next player in line after completing one lap of the circle.

➤ **Circle Weave:** This game is like Circle Relay except that players weave themselves in and out of the other players in the circle rather than running outside of them.

➤ **Leaping Circle Relay:** This variation is the same as Circle Relay except that players lie on the floor facing the center of the circle. Runners leap over those lying on the floor.

➤ **Everyone Goes:** This game is the same as Leaping Circle Relay except that once P1 passes P2, P2 follows P1. When P2 passes P3, then P3 follows P2. Each player follows the player behind her. When players return to their spots they sit down to see which group did it the quickest.

Cool-Down

This game is too vigorous to use as a cool-down unless players run at three-quarter speed.

20. Cumulative Relay

Number of players	Experience	Playing area
Teams of 3-6	All	Any flat surface

Recommended Equipment
One cone per team.

Setup
- ➤ Players stand in line behind a starting line.
- ➤ Place a cone 15 paces from the starting line.

Key Objective
To complete the relay as quickly as possible.

How to Play
The first player in line runs around the cone and back to the start line. When the player returns to the start line he hooks arms with the second player in line. The two players in line run around the cone, return to the start line, and hook up with the third player. Hookups continue until all players have been picked up. The team then switches directions, and the last player picked up is closest to the cone. Each time the team returns to the starting line, they drop off a player.

Safety Considerations
Be sure that the teams are far enough apart that they do not run into each other.

Cool-Down
This game is too vigorous to use as a cool-down.

21. Blindfolded Obstacle Relay

Number of players	Experience	Playing area
Teams of 3	All	Any flat surface

Recommended Equipment
Two blindfolds and six cones per group.

Setup
Each team lines up behind a start-finish line and has an obstacle course made of cones in front of them (each team has a similar course marked out).

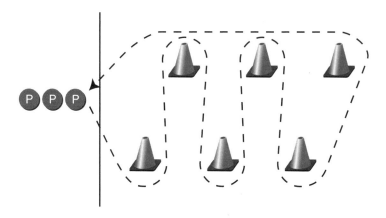

Key Objective
To complete the course as quickly as possible.

How to Play
Two of the players blindfold themselves. All three players stand behind the start-finish line. At the leader's signal to begin, the non-blindfolded player leads both of the blindfolded players around the obstacle course as quickly as possible. When the three players return to the finish line one of the blindfolded players gives the blindfold to the nonblindfolded player and leads the two blindfolded players through the course again. They go through the obstacle course a third time so that all three players have had an opportunity to lead and have twice completed the course blindfolded.

Safety Considerations

Be sure that there are no obstacles (walls or other stationary objects) that players might run into and that the teams' courses are far enough apart that players will not run into other competitors.

Instructional Tips

This activity can help teach trust in leadership.

Cool-Down

This game can work well as a cool-down if it is used not as a race but as a walking, trust-building activity.

22. Shuffle Run

Number of players	Experience	Playing area
Teams of 3	All	Any flat surface

Recommended Equipment

Two carpet pieces (large enough for players to put their feet on) and four cones per team.

Setup

Position the players behind a starting line. Each team lines up behind a start-finish line and has an obstacle course in front of them (each team has a similar course marked out).

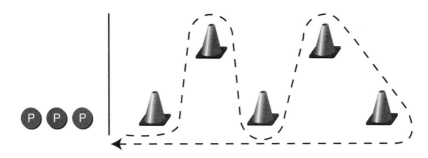

Key Objective

To complete the course as quickly as possible.

How to Play

All three players stand behind the start-finish line. At the leader's signal to begin, the first player shuffles through the obstacle course. When the shuffler returns to the start line the next player goes. Then the third player has a turn. The teams go through the course twice.

Variation

Shuffle Dribble: This race is like Shuffle Run, but players also dribble a basketball through the obstacle course.

Cool-Down

This game is too active to use as a cool-down.

23. Custodian Relay

Number of players	Experience	Playing area
Teams of 2-4	All	Open area with a hard, slippery floor (gymnasium, hallway)

Recommended Equipment
One towel per group.

Setup
Establish a start line and a turning line (on a volleyball court use the service line as a start line and the center line as the turning line). Line up teams behind the start line.

Key Objective
Each team tries to get to the turning line and back to the start line as quickly as possible.

How to Play
Each team lines up behind the start line with a towel. On the signal to start, the first player in line pushes the towel to the turning line and back to the start line as quickly as possible. Players hold onto the towel with both hands and push the towel along the floor. When the first player returns, the next player goes until everyone from the team has completed a run. Teams can repeat the up-and back trip several times.

Safety Considerations
Make sure that players have their hands well inside the towel to avoid floor burns.

Instructional Tips
This relay is an effective way to sweep the court floor.

Variation
Custodial Wheels: This relay can also be done using a scooter board instead of a towel.

Cool-Down
This activity is too vigorous to use as a cool-down.

24. Arch and Roll Relay

Number of players	Experience	Playing area
Several teams of 5-15	All	Any flat surface

Recommended Equipment
One round ball per team.

Setup
All team members line up in single file, one behind the other, facing the back of the player in front of them. The player in the back of the line begins with the ball.

Key Objective
To pass a ball under and over the team as quickly as possible.

How to Play
At the signal to begin, the back player rolls the ball forward between the legs of her teammates. The rest of the team helps hit the ball forward to the front player. When the player in the front gets the ball, the player in back moves to the front of the line. When the player in the front gets the ball, he passes it over his head to the player behind him. Each player in turn passes the ball overhead to the player behind her. When the back player gets the ball he rolls it forward between his teammates' legs. The front player passes the ball overhead. They continue until the back player is at the back of the line for the third time, at which point the team sits down. The first team to complete the relay and be seated is the winner.

Variation
Wobbly Arch and Roll Relay: This variation is the same as Arch and Roll Relay except that the teams use a football or rugby ball, which will not roll as smoothly between the players' legs.

Cool-Down
This game works great as a cool-down.

25. Exercise Relay

Number of players	Experience	Playing area
Teams of 5-8	All	Any flat surface

Recommended Equipment
None.

Setup
Players line up behind each other behind a starting line. A demonstration line is marked 10 paces in front of each team.

Key Objective
To complete a set of exercises (repeated 10 times each) before the other team does.

How to Play
At the signal to start, the first player runs to the demonstration line and does an exercise 10 times. The rest of the team does the same exercise 10 times with the demonstrator. When the demonstrator finishes the 10 exercises, he goes to the back of the line. The next player runs to the demonstration line and does a different exercise 10 times. The sequence continues until every player has demonstrated an exercise. The demonstrator cannot use an exercise previously used by a teammate.

Safety Considerations
This activity should be used only after a general warm-up.

Instructional Tips
You may want to list the exercises available but allow players to develop some creative new exercises.

Cool-Down
This activity does not work well as a cool-down.

CHAPTER 4

RACES

26. Heel-to-Toe Race

Number of players	Experience	Playing area
Any number	All	Any flat surface

Recommended Equipment
None.

Setup
All players stand beside each other behind a starting line. Designate a turning line 20 paces away.

Key Objective
To run as quickly as possible from the start line to a turning line and back to the start line.

How to Play
On the leader's signal to run, players race as quickly as possible to the turning line and back. When players run they must place the heel of the lead foot against the toe of the back foot and then move the back foot in front so that the heel of that foot touches the toe of the new back foot.

Safety Considerations
Be sure that the start-finish line and turning line are far enough from walls so that if players fall they will not injure themselves by falling against a wall.

Variation
Backward Heel-to-Toe Race: Players race as they do in Heel-to-Toe Race except that they run in a backward direction.

Cool-Down
This activity can work well as a cool-down if players perform for a shorter distance and do not race.

27. Over and Under

Number of players	Experience	Playing area
Teams of 5-10	All	Gymnasium or large room

Recommended Equipment
One ball (or rubber chicken or beanbag or whatever) per group.

Setup
Each team lines up in a row with players facing the back of the player in front of them.

Key Objective
To see how quickly players can pass a ball to the back and front again.

How to Play
The player in the front passes the ball over her head to the player behind her. The next player in line passes the ball between his legs to the player behind him. The over-and-under pattern continues until the ball reaches the player at the back of the line. The player at the back of the line passes the ball forward over the head of the player in front of her. The next player in line passes the ball between the legs of the player in front of him. The over-and-under pattern continues until the ball reaches the player at the front of the line. The team repeats the process for a specified number of times and sees how quickly they can do it.

Variations
➤ **Team Over and Under:** Divide the group in half. One team stands in a tight circle with one player holding the ball. The player with the ball throws the ball anywhere in the gymnasium and then runs around her group in the tight circle. The other team runs to get the ball and forms a line with each player facing the back of the teammates in front of her. The first player who gets the ball passes it over his head to the player behind him. The next player puts the ball between her legs to the player behind her. Play continues over and under all the players until the last player in line gets it and yells, "Stop." At the command to stop, the team

whose player was running the circles counts the number of laps their runner completed. The team that was in the line moves into a tight circle and throws the ball. The teams repeat several times to see which group can do the most cumulative laps.

➤ **Continuous Over and Under:** After the front player passes the ball she runs to the back of the line. Other players follow, first passing the ball and then running to the back of the line. They see how quickly they can perform 10 complete rotations. This game can also be done passing forward.

Cool-Down

This race works great as a cool-down.

28. Everybody Over and Under

Number of players	Experience	Playing area
Teams of 4-10	All	Any flat surface

Recommended Equipment
None.

Setup
Players position themselves on the floor on all fours (on both hands and both knees), in a line (like railway ties) approximately one step apart.

Key Objective
To get everybody on the team over and under everyone else on the team as quickly as possible.

How to Play
On the signal to begin, the last player in line goes over the second-to-last player, under the third-to-last player, over the fourth-to-last player, and so on until she reaches the front of the line, where she positions herself on all fours. Once the last player has gone over the second-to-last player, the second-to-last player goes over the third-to-last player, under the fourth-to-last player, and so on until he reaches the front of the line. They continue this sequence until they complete a specified number of complete cycles (four to eight).

Safety Considerations
Players should avoid standing on each other's hands or otherwise hurting each other as they go over and under.

Variation
Circular Everybody Over and Under: Players position themselves in a circle on all fours one step apart with their heads facing inside the circle. Each group completes the race as in Everybody Over and Under except that they perform it in a circle and complete the circle four to eight times.

Cool-Down
This activity can work as a cool-down if the leader uses a longer line, has larger groups, has players go one at a time, and has players do it only once each.

29. Caterpillar Race

Number of players	Experience	Playing area
Teams of 3-15	All	Any flat surface

Recommended Equipment
None.

Setup
Players line up single file in a row facing each other's back behind a starting line. Establish a finish line 30 paces away.

Key Objective
To complete the race as quickly as possible.

How to Play
Players lean forward and hold on to the ankles of the player in front of them. On the signal to begin, the team advances forward toward the finish line.

Instructional Tips
This activity is a difficult warm-up. It may help the players to call out left and right to indicate which foot everyone is moving.

Variation
Caterpillar Bend: This race is the same as Caterpillar Race except that the team does a figure 8 around two cones. Players will have lots of laughs as the caterpillar tries to bend around the cones.

Cool-Down
This race is a little too strenuous to serve as a cool-down.

30. Butt Crawl

Number of players	Experience	Playing area
Teams of 3-8	All	Any smooth floor

Recommended Equipment
None.

Setup
Players sit behind a start line with their feet wrapped around the player in front of them and on top of his legs. Establish a finish line 15 paces away.

Key Objective
To complete the race as quickly as possible.

How to Play
At the signal to start, players, in unison, rock from side to side and move forward as a team to the finish line. When the front player touches the finish line the team has completed the race.

Variation
Backward Butt Crawl: This race is like the Butt Crawl, but teams line up backward and move backward.

Cool-Down
This activity is too strenuous for use as a cool-down.

31. Octopus

Number of players	Experience	Playing area
Teams of 2	Experienced	Any flat surface

Recommended Equipment
None.

Setup
Establish a start line and a finish line approximately 30 paces apart. Partners of similar size and weight stand back to back at the start line and lock arms together.

Key Objective
To get from the start line to the finish line as quickly as possible.

How to Play
At the signal to start, one partner leans forward, turns, and stands up straight. This movement puts the partner closer to the finish line. The partner then leans forward, picks up her partner, turns, and stands up straight. This movement puts the other partner closer to the finish line. The partners continue until they have rocked all the way to the finish line.

Safety Considerations
Partners should not lean forward so far that they risk falling head over heels.

Cool-Down
This activity works well as a cool-down if the speed element is removed.

32. Snakeskin

Number of players	Experience	Playing area
Teams of 3-13	All	Any flat surface

Recommended Equipment
None.

Setup
Players stand two paces apart in a long line facing each other's backs.

Key Objective
To skin the snake a set number of times.

How to Play
The first player in the line lies down straight with arms pointed forward.

Player 2 (P2) runs over (with feet beside the player) P1 and lies down in front of the first player's hands. P3 runs immediately behind P2 over P1 and then over P2. P3 then lies down in front of P2. The players continue until everyone has run over P1. The leader can have each team repeat the sequence a specified number of times.

Safety Considerations
Players who are lying down must keep a long, narrow position to avoid being stepped on. Players who are running must pay close attention to the players lying down to avoid stepping on them.

Variations
➤ **Front Crawl:** This race is the same as Snakeskin except that the back player crawls on hands and knees (better suited for a grass surface than a hard gymnasium floor) underneath her team, which is standing in a line with their feet spread. When the back player reaches the front, she stands up and spreads her feet so that the next player can go between them. Once the back player has gone underneath the second-to-last player, that player goes

on hands and knees and crawls underneath the team. Players go through the line a specified number of times. Players could also do a front crawl until everyone has completed the event once and then do it in reverse order with a backward crawl to get everyone back to the original position.

➤ **Slalom Skier:** This race is the same as Snakeskin except that players kneel at right angles to each other and the other players jump or do two-footed hops over the kneeling players. For safety, make sure that players who are kneeling stay low to the ground and far from the last player they jumped or hopped over so that their teammates do not jump or hop into them.

➤ **Frogs and Snakes:** This race is like Snakeskin except that the second player in line leapfrogs over a kneeling first player and then takes a position with legs straddled three paces in front of the first player. The third player leapfrogs over the first player, crawls like a snake between the second player's legs, and then sets up to be leapfrogged over.

Cool-Down
This activity works well as a cool-down if players go at three-quarter speed and perform for a set distance, not a time limit.

33. Over, Under, Around

Number of players	Experience	Playing area
Teams of 3	All	Any flat surface

Recommended Equipment
None.

Setup
Players stand in teams of three and wait for the teacher to announce the challenge.

Key Objective
To complete the challenge as quickly as possible.

How to Play
Players are instructed to time how quickly they can fulfill the instructions given by the teacher. For example, the teacher states, "Over, under, around, go!" Each player, one at a time, must travel over her group, under her group, and around her group, until all three players have fulfilled the instructions. The group then sits and yells, "Done!" The first group to complete the task successfully is the winner.

Safety Considerations
Encourage players to select the safest way, which is usually the quickest way, to solve the challenge.

Instructional Tips
The leader can give the teams time to determine the quickest way of succeeding at the challenge before calling, "Go!"

Variations
➤ **Mass Over, Under, and Around:** Instead of teams of three, make the teams larger by adding another one to five players.
➤ **Backward Over, Under, and Around:** The "runner" must travel with his back in the direction he is traveling.

Cool-Down
This game is too active to be used as a cool-down.

34. Hole in One

Number of players	Experience	Playing area
Teams of 7 or more	All	Any flat surface

Recommended Equipment
A piece of cardboard tubing (carpet rolls obtained free at a carpet store) cut into lengths of approximately 1 yard or 1 meter for every one to four players and one golf ball per team.

Setup
Establish a start line on which the last players in a line stand. Players stand in teams of one to four players per tube and all hold onto their tubes horizontally to form a long tube. The last player for each long tube has a golf ball.

Key Objective
To see how far a team can go in 4 minutes while keeping the golf ball from falling out of the tubes.

How to Play
On the signal to begin, the golf ball is placed in the last tube. When the ball leaves that tube, the players holding the tube run to the front of the line and position their tube so that the ball can go through their tube when it gets that far. Play continues for 4 minutes, and players see how far they can go. If the ball falls out of the tubes players must return to the start line and try again.

Instructional Tips
Players must control the speed of the ball so that the players at the back of the line have adequate time to get to the front of the line.

Variation
Two-Tube Hole in One: Each team of players is given only two tubes. The game is similar to Hole in One, but because each team uses only two tubes the game is very fast.

Cool-Down
This game works well as a cool-down, especially if the line is long.

35. Rat Race

Number of players	Experience	Playing area
Any number, but an odd number works best	All	Any flat surface

Recommended Equipment
Four cones and a CD or tape player with fun and lively music.

Setup
Set up four cones to create a safe track (possibly the size of a volleyball court) for players to jog around.

Key Objective
To jog and find a partner at breaks in the activity.

How to Play
Players are positioned outside the cones. Play some fast-paced music while the players jog around the cones. When the music stops, "rats" move forward (they are not allowed to move backward against the flow of the rat race) to find a partner. They take a break by sitting back to back inside the cones. After 4 seconds, any player without a partner does five star jumps. Music and jogging resume.

Safety Considerations
To avoid running into each other, players may move in only one direction.

Instructional Tips
The pace of the music will affect the speed of the jog.

Cool-Down
The race works well as a cool-down by using slower music and having students do the star jumps in slow motion.

36. Swamp Pass

Number of players	Experience	Playing area
Groups of 4-8	All	Any flat, smooth surface

Recommended Equipment

One small piece of carpet for each player and one extra piece. The carpet pieces should be large enough for a player to stand on with both feet.

Setup

Players stand behind each other and behind a start line, each on a piece of carpet. The last player in line stands on two pieces of carpet (one for each foot).

Key Objective

To pass each other five times as quickly as possible.

How to Play

The group remains stationary except for the last player in line, who shuffles on the carpet pieces past the rest of her team until she is in the front of the line. When the shuffler is in the front of the line she places both feet on one piece of carpet and passes the extra carpet back down the line to the player at the end of the line. (For extra fun players can pass the carpet back so that it takes a path over the head of the first player, between the legs of the second player, over the head of the third player, and so on.) When the player at the end of the line gets the extra piece of carpet, he shuffles by the rest of his team until he is in the front of the line. The sequence continues until everyone has shuffled five times.

Variation

Multishuffle Swamp Pass: This variation is played the same way as Swamp Pass is played except that two or three extra pieces of carpet are used and several players are shuffling to the front at the same time.

Cool-Down

Works well as a cool-down but challenge the players to repeat the activity 3-4 times taking twice as long as when they did the activity as quickly as possible.

37. Leapfrog

Number of players	Experience	Playing area
Teams of 2	Experienced	Any flat surface

Recommended Equipment
None.

Setup
Players partner up with another player, and pairs stand beside each other behind a starting line.

Key Objective
To complete 10 leapfrogs each as quickly as possible.

How to Play
At the leader's signal to begin, players leapfrog over their partners and in turn their partners leapfrog over them. They complete this sequence 10 times. When the partners have each done 10 leapfrogs, they sit down where they are to indicate that they are done.

Safety Considerations
Players should leapfrog in a straight line to avoid bumping into players leapfrogging on either side of them.

Instructional Tips
Low obstacles are easier to jump over than high obstacles. As a leader you may wish to allow any height or specify a certain height.

Variations
- ➤ **Leapfrog, Leapfrog, Snake, Snake:** This race is like Leapfrog except that after each player has leapfrogged his partner, he crawls between his partner's legs once. The players then each do another leap, then another snake, and so on, continuing until each player has completed five leapfrogs and five snakes.
- ➤ **Leapfrog, Leapfrog, Octopus, Octopus:** This race is like Leapfrog except that after players leapfrog over their partners, they do an octopus spin. Players then each do a leapfrog, then an octopus spin, and so on. To perform an octopus spin, players stand back to back and lock arms. One partner leans forward, picks up her partner, turns, and stands up straight, which moves the partner

forward and changes direction 180 degrees. The other partner does the same. The race continues until each player has completed five leapfrogs and five octopuses.

Cool-Down

This activity works well as a cool-down if the race element is eliminated.

38. Le Mans 24-Lap Tandem Race

Number of players	Experience	Playing area
Teams of 3	Experienced	Any floor

Recommended Equipment

One scooter per team.

Setup

➤ Set up an obstacle course as a racetrack, perhaps with a cone that racers must pass by at each corner of a volleyball court.

➤ Each team sets up their scooter at the finish line and stands five paces back.

Key Objective

To complete 24 laps as quickly as possible.

How to Play

At the leader's signal, two teammates run to the scooter. One player sits on the scooter, and the second player pushes the seated player around the course. When the scooter completes one lap, the seated player dismounts, the pusher sits on the scooter, the third teammate pushes the seated player around the course for one lap, and so on. The first team to complete 24 laps is the winner.

Safety Considerations

Players need to watch that their fingers do not go under the wheels of the scooters. Players should wear helmets for safety and realism.

Instructional Tips

The leader may want to appoint several pit-stop areas to avoid congestion at one place along the track when racers switch spots.

Cool-Down

This race is too vigorous to use as a cool-down.

CHAPTER 5

PARACHUTE GAMES

39. Team Run

Number of players	Experience	Playing area
Groups of 5-25	All	Any flat surface

Recommended Equipment
Parachute (or large tarp) for each group.

Setup
All players stand outside the parachute and hold onto the outer edge with their right hands.

Key Objective
To complete different movements as a team while all players hold the parachute.

How to Play
The leader calls for different ways of moving as a team, and the team follows the instructions while holding the parachute. For example, all players jog, hop on one foot, take lunge steps, or hop on both feet.

Safety Considerations
To prevent players from falling and hurting themselves, do not let the team go too fast.

Instructional Tips
The whole team has to work at the same pace to make the movements work.

Variation
Team Sit-Ups: Players sit around the parachute with the parachute draped over their legs. One side leans back to the ground and then pulls up with the assistance of players on the opposite side of the parachute. Then players to the left of the players that completed their sit-up lean back and are pulled back up. The action continues in a clockwise direction until everyone has completed 20 sit-ups.

Cool-Down
This game works well as a cool-down if the speed of movements is not fast.

40. Under Frog

Number of players	Experience	Playing area
2 groups of 4-10	All	Any flat surface

Recommended Equipment
Two parachutes or tarps.

Setup
Two teams hold their respective parachutes and stand beside each other.

Key Objective
To have one team go under the other team's parachute and alternate this process for a set time or distance.

How to Play
By lifting and extending their arms, one team lifts the parachute into a mushroom shape. The other team runs underneath the lifted parachute while holding onto their parachute. After they pass completely under the other team's parachute, they lift their parachute into a mushroom shape and the other team goes underneath their parachute. Teams continue to alternate lifting their parachute and going under the other team's parachute for a preset time limit or number of laps around the playing area.

Instructional Tips
Teams will need to create a lane underneath their parachute for the other team to cross underneath it.

Cool-Down
Because of the lofting of the parachutes, this activity works well as a cool-down.

41. High Rollers

Number of players	Experience	Playing area
Teams of 5-25	All	Any flat surface

Recommended Equipment
One parachute or large tarp per team.

Setup
All teammates stand around their parachute and hold the parachute with both hands in front of them.

Key Objective
To see how many laps a ball can go around the parachute in a set time.

How to Play
Players alternate putting their hands on the ground and then lifting their hands above their heads in an organized manner. This action produces a wavelike movement of the parachute, which pushes the ball around the parachute. Players will need to control the speed of the ball to complete the most laps without rolling the ball off the parachute. If the ball rolls off they should throw it back on and continue counting their laps.

Instructional Tips
To get the maximum warm-up benefit, players must put their hands on the ground and then above their heads.

Cool-Down
This game works well as a cool-down if teams try to achieve a certain number of laps in a specific but longer time. For example, they could attempt to complete six laps in 60 seconds.

PART II

SPORT-SPECIFIC WARM-UP AND COOL-DOWN GAMES

CHAPTER 6

BADMINTON

42. Bird Juggle

Number of players	Experience	Playing area
1	Experienced	Flat area, preferably with badminton courts

Recommended Equipment
One badminton racket and one bird for each player.

Setup
Players position themselves in a scatter formation around the playing area, far enough apart that they will not hit someone else with their rackets.

Key Objective
To see how long a player can continuously hit a bird.

How to Play
Each player hits the bird approximately 1 yard or 1 meter high. While maintaining the same grip the player hits the bird first on the forehand side of the racket, then on the backhand side, then on the forehand side, and so on.

Safety Considerations
Players should stay in their positions so that they do not hit anyone else with their rackets.

Instructional Tips
This activity develops proficiency in gripping the racket.

Variations
- ➤ **Low-Bird Juggle:** This game is the same as Bird Juggle except that players should try to keep the bird close to the racket.
- ➤ **Walking Bird Juggle:** This variation is the same as Bird Juggle except that players keep the bird going as they walk around the outside of their badminton court. For safety, warn them not to walk into the badminton posts or other players.
- ➤ **Bird Trap:** Have players place a bird on the floor. Using the side edge of the racket, they pick up the bird. They then toss the bird several paces away, pick it up, and toss it again.

➤ **Bird Flick:** Have players pair up and stand three paces apart. Place a bird on the floor by one of the players. One partner puts his racket beside the bird and flicks it up to his partner. See how many successful flicks can be made with 20 tries.

➤ **Bird Catcher:** Players hit a bird in the air and catch it with the racket. This activity works best when the racket face can come down beside the bird, decelerate, and then come under it. Players hit the bird a few paces away each time.

➤ **Two-Bird Rally:** Have players pair up and stand four paces apart. Each player holds a bird. At their own signal to start, they see how long they can pass two birds between each other.

Cool-Down

All of these games work well as cool-downs with the exception of Two-Bird Rally. To make that variation work as a cool-down, players should move back a couple of steps.

43. Thread the Button

Number of players	Experience	Playing area
Teams of 5-8	Experienced	Half a badminton court

Recommended Equipment
A badminton racket for each player and one bird per group.

Setup
Players stand around the edge of half a badminton court.

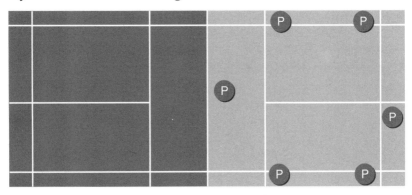

Key Objective
All players must make a successful pass to a different player.

How to Play
Players must pass the bird to someone not immediately beside them. When a player has received and passed the bird, she puts her racket in the air to indicate that she has received a pass. Players try to go around two or more times and must hit the bird to a different player each time it comes to them. They play until a pass is not successful or until a player passes the bird a second time to the same player before passing it to every player at least once.

Safety Considerations
Players need to communicate who is receiving the bird so that they do not strike each other with their rackets.

Instructional Tips
Communication, racket control, placement, and observation are important in this drill.

Variations

➤ **Two-Bird Thread the Button:** This variation is the same as Thread the Button except that players use two birds at the same time. Players must communicate and be aware of the other bird while playing the first bird.

➤ **Buttonhole:** A player takes a position in the middle of the other players. This player passes a bird out to a player on the outside, who passes it back to the middle player, who passes it back to the next player, and so on until everyone has successfully passed the bird. Following one complete circle, another player takes the middle position so that everyone gets a turn.

➤ **Broken Buttonhole:** A player takes the middle position. The players on the outside pass the bird to each other. The player in the middle tries to intercept the bird or wait for an incomplete pass, at which time the last player to contact the bird switches with the player in the middle. Players must be careful to avoid hitting each other with their rackets (the player in the middle can use a pool noodle instead of a racket).

➤ **Buttonhole Sit-Up:** This variation is played as Buttonhole is played except that all players are seated. When a player on the outside passes the bird to the player in the middle, all players do a quick sit-up. They see how many consecutive sit-ups they can do before someone makes an errant pass.

Cool-Down

This game works well as a cool-down except for the more active variations (Two-Bird Thread the Button, Broken Buttonhole, and Buttonhole Sit-Up).

44. Clear, Drop

Number of players	Experience	Playing area
Partners (twice as many pairs as there are courts)	Experienced	Badminton court

Recommended Equipment
A badminton racket for each player and one bird per pair of players.

Setup
One player stands by the net with a bird in hand, and the other player stands opposite the net in the back of the badminton court. They play on half the width of a court.

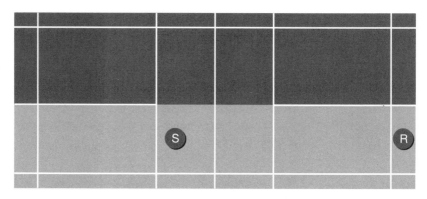

Key Objective
To see how long players can successfully pass the bird close to the back of the court (ideally between the doubles backcourt service line and the end line) and close to the front of the court (between the short service line and the net).

How to Play
The player at the net clears the bird to the player in the back. The player in the back returns a drop shot to the player in the front. They see how long they can successfully continue this pattern.

Safety Considerations
If more than one pair of players are doing the drill on the same court, players need to be careful that they do not hit each other.

Instructional Tips

Emphasize proper distance, trajectory, and speed of shots.

Variations

➤ Many variations on Clear, Drop involve more movement, including the following:

Clear, Clear, Drop

Clear, Drop, Drop

Clear, Clear, Drop, Drop

Clear, Clear, Clear, Drop

➤ **Doubles Clear, Drop:** Each variation can also be played with pairs (one at the net and the other at the back of the court). Although playing in pairs includes more players, it reduces the movement of each player.

Cool-Down

All variations work well as cool-downs, particularly if the clears are high and players do not use too many drop shots.

45. Long Cross and Drop

Number of players	Experience	Playing area
Pairs	Experienced	Badminton court

Recommended Equipment
A badminton racket for each player and one bird for each pair of players.

Setup
One player stands at the net with a bird in hand, and the other player stands on the other side of the net in the back opposite corner.

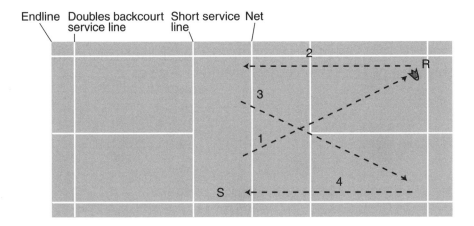

Key Objective
To see how long players can successfully pass the bird close to the back of the court (ideally between the doubles backcourt service line and the end line) and close to the front of the court (between the short service line and the net).

How to Play
The front player hits the bird crosscourt and deep into the opposite back corner. The back player returns a drop shot straight down the line. The front player returns the bird crosscourt and deep into the opposite back corner. The back player returns a drop shot straight down the line. Players see how many times they can successfully complete this sequence.

Instructional Tips

Emphasize proper placement, trajectory, and speed of shots.

Variations

➤ Among the many variations on Long Cross and Drop are the following sequences:

Long Cross, Drop, Drop

Short Cross, Drop, Drop

Short Cross, Drop, Short Cross, Drop

Long Cross, Clear, Drop

➤ **Doubles Long Cross and Drop:** Each variation can also be played with pairs (one at the net and the other at the back of the court). Although playing in pairs includes more players, it reduces the movement of each player.

Cool-Down

All variations work well as cool-downs, particularly if the clears are high and players do not use too many drop shots.

46. Next-in-Line Badminton

Number of players	Experience	Playing area
6-10 per court	Experienced	Badminton court

Recommended Equipment
One badminton racket for each player and one bird per court.

Setup
A server and a receiver are on the court in singles badminton position. The remaining players line up behind the back end line.

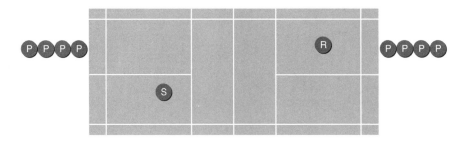

Key Objective
To score points by landing the bird in the opponent's court.

How to Play
Four players from each team line up behind the court. One player from each team stands on the court. One player serves the bird and then goes to the side of the court and to the back of the line. The front player in the line goes quickly onto the court. They play with regular badminton rules.

Safety Considerations
Players should leave the court by the side to avoid colliding with their teammates moving in from the back of the court.

Variation
Side Subs Badminton: One player is on the court, a teammate stands behind the court, and two other teammates stand on either side of the court. They play using regular badminton rules except that after

a player hits the bird he goes to a spot vacated by a teammate on the sidelines. Players on the side must communicate which of them is in the most strategic spot to enter the game. Every player must contact the bird before any player can contact the bird a second time.

Cool-Down
This game works well as a cool-down activity.

47. Five-Player Continuous Rally

Number of players	Experience	Playing area
At least 5	Experienced	Badminton court

Recommended Equipment
One badminton racket for each player and one bird per court.

Setup
A server and a receiver are on the court in a singles badminton position. The remaining players line up beside the court.

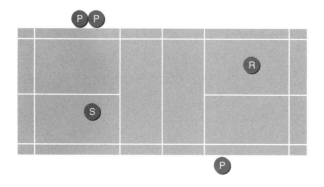

Key Objective
To see how long players can maintain a rally.

How to Play
Players use regular badminton rules except that once players hit the bird, they must exit the court on the right side and go to the opposite court. The serving side should begin with the server and at least two players waiting on the sideline to come onto the court. The other side should have a receiver and at least one player waiting on the sideline to come onto the court. Players rotate counterclockwise and try to maintain a rally as long as possible.

Safety Considerations
Make sure that no debris (extra birds or clothing items) is lying around that might cause players to slip when running to the other side of the court.

Instructional Tips

The higher the bird, the more time teammates have to get onto the court and play a successful return shot.

Cool-Down

This game works well as a cool-down. If playing with five players is too vigorous, using more players slows the pace.

48. Upset

Number of players	Experience	Playing area
At least 3 per court	Experienced	Badminton court

Recommended Equipment
One badminton racket per player and one bird per court.

Setup
A server and a receiver are on the court in a singles badminton position. The remaining player or players line up beside the court.

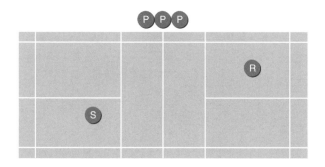

Key Objective
Each player tries to stay on the court as long as possible.

How to Play
Regular badminton rules are used. When a player loses a rally she goes to the back of the line of players waiting to get on, and the first player in line enters the court and prepares to receive service.

Safety Considerations
Make sure that the line of players on the side is far enough away from the court that players on the court do not hit them with a racket or run into them.

Variations
➤ **Doubles Upset:** Players play as they do in Upset, but they use doubles rules with two players leaving and entering the court after each rally.

➤ **Team Upset:** Players play as they do in Upset, but each side has their own line of replacement players. Players keep score as they do in regular badminton. Additionally, players who score 4 points in a row change places with a replacement player.

Cool-Down

This game works well as a cool-down activity.

49. Cooperative Net Game

Number of players	Experience	Playing area
2	Experienced	Badminton court

Recommended Equipment
A badminton racket for each player and one bird per pair of players.

Setup
Two players stand on opposite sides of the net at one side of the court. One of the players holds a bird.

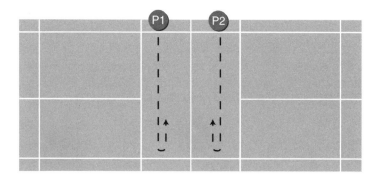

Key Objective
To see how long players can hit the bird to each other while they move from one side of the court to the other and back again.

How to Play
The player with the bird gently hits a short shot over the net to her partner. The partner hits a gentle return. Players continue hitting the bird to each other as they try to move to the other side of the court and back again.

Safety Considerations
To prevent players from hitting each other, rackets may not cross the plane of the net.

Instructional Tips
Players should contact the bird early to avoid having to hit the bird too far up.

Variations

➤ **Competitive Net Game:** One player stands on either side of the net just behind the short service line in a doubles serve–serve receive position. The game can also be played on a narrow (half) court to accommodate more players. The objective of this game is to have the bird land on the opponent's side of the court. Regular badminton rules apply with two significant differences:

1. Only a short serve into the regular court is permitted.

2. Following the serve, the short service line becomes the back of the court. All play must occur inside the very short court.

➤ **Competitive Two-Zone Net Game:** This game is a more difficult version of Competitive Net Game. Mark two squares two steps across on either side of the court by the net. After the service, players can score only if the bird lands in either of their opponent's two zones.

➤ **Half Cooperative Net Game (or Competitive Net Game):** Play these games on a narrow (half) court.

➤ **Doubles Net Game:** Play Cooperative Net Game or any of the variations with two players per side.

Cool-Down

Cooperative Net Game and Doubles Net Game will work well as cool-downs, but the other variations are too demanding.

50. Cat in the Middle

Number of players	Experience	Playing area
3	Expert	Badminton court without a net

Recommended Equipment

A badminton racket for each player (the cat in the middle could use a pool noodle to make things safer) and one bird per group of players.

Setup

Use no net and have the "cat" stand between the short service lines. The other two players stand on either side of the court. Players use a long, narrow (half) court.

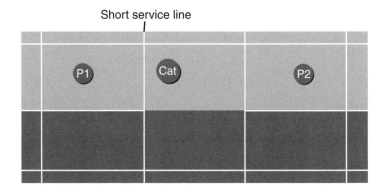

Short service line

Key Objective

To hit high, deep clears that prevent the cat from intercepting the bird.

How to Play

One player serves an underhand clear to begin play. The cat tries to catch the bird, and the two other players hit the bird over the cat. When the cat intercepts the bird or a player hits out of bounds, the errant player changes places with the cat.

Safety Considerations

To prevent players from striking each other with their rackets, provide the cat with a pool noodle or establish a safety line one step back from the short service line that players may not enter with their bodies.

Instructional Tips

Encourage players to hit long, high clears.

Variation

Cat Badminton: Players observe regular badminton rules but replace the net with a cat or cats in the middle, between the two short service lines. The cat cannot intercept the serve (the serve must go over imaginary net). No drive shots or smashes are permitted (for the safety of the cat), and the bird must land behind the short service line and in the court. Whoever loses the rally changes places with the cat.

Cool-Down

This game works well as a cool-down.

51. Driving

Number of players	Experience	Playing area
Pairs	Expert	Badminton court

Recommended Equipment

A badminton racket for each player and one bird per pair of players.

Setup

Two players stand on opposite sides of the net at approximately midcourt.

Key Objective

To see how many successive drive shots players can achieve.

How to Play

A player with the bird drives a low, flat, hard shot to her partner on the opposite side of the net. Her partner returns the shot with a drive shot. Players try to see how long they can continue hitting drive shots at each other.

Instructional Tips

Players start by hitting forehand to forehand, then backhand to backhand, and then a mix of shots.

Variation

Four-Wheel Driving: Have four players on the court, two on each side. One doubles team begins and hits all their drives crosscourt. The other team responds by driving all the birds down the line. Teams alternate so that each team has the opportunity to hit drives crosscourt and straight.

Cool-Down

This activity is too stressful to use as a cool-down.

52. Short and Long Game

Number of players	Experience	Playing area
Pairs	Expert	Badminton court

Recommended Equipment
A badminton racket for each player and one bird per pair of players.

Setup
One player stands on either side of the net just behind the short service line in a doubles serve–serve receive position. The game can also be played on a narrow (half) court to accommodate more players.

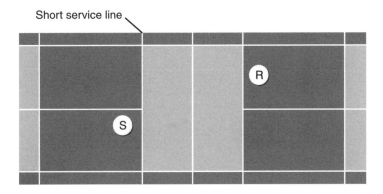

Key Objective
To have the bird land on the opponent's court.

How to Play
Regular badminton rules apply with two significant differences:

1. Only a short serve into the regular court is permitted.
2. Following the serve, the short service line becomes the back of the court. The bird must land inside the very short court or inside the area in the back of the court.

Variations
➤ **Long Game:** This variation is like Short and Long Game except that after the service only the backcourt is considered in. The game requires good hitting ability. If players have too much difficulty keeping the bird inside the backcourt, add a line closer to the net to increase the size of the backcourt.

➤ **Doubles Short, Long, and Wide:** Players play doubles as they do in Short and Long Game, but after the service the two side areas between the singles sideline and the doubles sideline are also in play.

Cool-Down

This game and its variations work well for a cool-down when two players play each side (with the exception of Long Game, which can be played with one player on a side).

53. Played by the Book

Number of players	Experience	Playing area
Pairs	Expert	Badminton court

Recommended Equipment
A badminton racket for each player and one bird per pair of players.

Setup
One player stands on either side of the net just behind the short service line in a doubles serve–serve receive position. The game can also be played on a narrow (half) court to accommodate more players.

Key Objective
To learn to add precision and deception to shots.

How to Play
Regular badminton rules are used with the exception that players must follow a prescribed shot pattern, that is, clear, clear, drop. Shooting precisely and using deception to move the opponent side to side are essential to success

Variations
Patterns include the following:

Clear, Drop, Drop

Clear, Clear, Clear, Drop

Clear, Clear, Drop, Drop

Clear, Drop, Drop, Drop

Clear, Clear, Clear, Clear, Drop

Clear, Clear, Clear, Drop, Drop

Clear, Clear, Drop, Drop, Drop

Clear, Drop, Drop, Drop, Drop

Cool-Down
This game works well as a cool-down, particularly when played as a doubles game.

54. Narrow Clear, Smash, Drop

Number of players	Experience	Playing area
Pairs	Expert	Badminton court

Recommended Equipment
A badminton racket for each player and one bird per pair of players.

Setup
One player stands on either side of the net. The player with the bird stands close to the short service line, and the player receiving stands near the back of the court.

Key Objective
To see how long players can keep the sequence going.

How to Play
The starting player hits a deep clear to his partner. The receiver smashes the bird back. The starter returns a drop shot off the smash return. Players continue the sequence until one of them makes an errant shot.

Safety Considerations
If the clear is not very deep, players should protect their eyes from a smashed bird into the face.

Cool-Down
This activity is a bit too aggressive for a cool-down unless half-speed smashes are used.

CHAPTER 7

BASEBALL

55. Jog Toss

Number of players	Experience	Playing area
Groups of 5 or more	All	Any flat surface

Recommended Equipment
One baseball per player.

Setup
The group stands in a circle with players facing the back of the player in front of them, approximately two to five paces apart. Each player has a ball.

Key Objective
To see how many times the group can pass the balls before someone drops a pass.

How to Play
Players begin to jog slowly around a circle (a group of 12 or more players could run around the bases). On the signal, "Ready, Now," players simultaneously toss their balls in the air and then catch the ball thrown in the air by the player in front of them.

Safety Considerations
Players need to be aware of where they are running so that they do not run into the player in front of them or trip over a base.

Instructional Tips
➤ Players must learn to throw the ball to the right height, neither so low that catching it is difficult nor so high that the throw slows the team's jogging pace.
➤ Players can run clockwise or counterclockwise.

Variations
➤ **Jog Double Toss:** This variation is the same as Jog Toss except that the throw must be caught by a player who is two positions back rather than one position back.
➤ **Jog Forward Toss:** This game is like Jog Toss or Jog Double Toss except that players throw the ball forward.

- ➤ **Fowl Throw:** This game is like Jog Toss or its variations except that players throw rubber chickens.
- ➤ **Multisport Jog Toss:** This game is like Jog Toss or its variations except that players use other balls (basketballs or footballs).

Cool-Down
This game is a great cool-down.

56. Short Relay

Number of players	Experience	Playing area
Teams of 3	Experienced	Any flat surface

Recommended Equipment
One ball per group and a glove for each player.

Setup
Two players stand 20 paces apart, and the third player stands between them.

Key Objective
To count how many passes players can make in 1 minute.

How to Play
A player on one end throws the ball to the player in the middle (relay player), who turns and relays (throws) the ball to the third player. The third player returns the ball to the middle player, who turns and relays the ball to the original thrower. Players count how many passes they make in 1 minute and then switch the order so that all players have an opportunity to be the relay player.

Cool-Down
The game works well as a cool-down by removing the time element. Players should complete the drill 10 times and then switch positions so that all players have an opportunity to be the relay player.

57. Pop-Up One Bounce

Number of players	Experience	Playing area
Teams of 2	Experienced	Any flat field

Recommended Equipment
A glove for each player and one ball for each pair of players.

Setup
Players stand 15 paces apart, and one player has a ball.

Key Objective
To see how many consecutive catches a pair of players can make.

How to Play
The player with the ball tosses a high pop-up fly ball to her partner. The fielder catches the ball and tosses a one-bounce throw back to his partner. Players switch roles every 10 passes and count how many consecutive catches they can make.

Cool-Down
This drill works well as a cool-down, especially if players throw at half speed.

58. Hot Potato Baseball

Number of players	Experience	Playing area
Teams of 3-8	Experienced	Any flat surface

Recommended Equipment
One ball per group and a baseball glove for each player.

Setup
Players stand in a circle facing each other.

Key Objective
To see how long the group can keep the ball off the ground by hitting the ball to each other off their gloves.

How to Play
One player with the ball hits the ball off her glove to another player. The next player hits the ball off his glove to another player. Players may only hit the ball to another player and cannot hit the ball twice in a row.

Safety Considerations
The ball is hard so players should watch it carefully so that it does not hit them in the face.

Cool-Down
This drill is a little too intense to serve as a cool-down.

59. Two-a-Side Fantasy Baseball

Number of players	Experience	Playing area
2 teams of 2	Experienced	Any flat field

Recommended Equipment
Two cones, one bat, one ball, and two baseball gloves.

Setup
Place two cones 10 paces apart and a batting line 20 paces from the cones. The first fielder (F1) cannot go behind the cones. F2 cannot go in front of the cones.

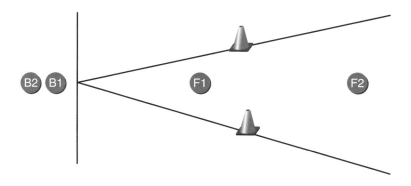

Key Objective
To score more runs than the opponents do.

How to Play
Batter 1 (B1) tosses the ball to himself and hits the ball between the cones. The batter is out if he

➤ hits a ball caught by one of the fielders before the ball contacts the ground,

➤ hits a foul ball (outside the imaginary line from home base over the two cones), or

➤ swings at a tossed ball and misses.

When a batter is out his partner goes up to bat. When they are both out, an inning is over and the fielders and batters switch sides. A ball hit along the ground and caught by F1 counts as a strike (three consecutive strikes also count as one out). A ball hit past the cones along the ground counts as a single (players must keep track of base runners in their heads). A ball that lands past the cones that F2 catches off the bounce counts as a double. A ball that lands past the cones and rolls past F2 counts as a triple. A ball that lands past F2 counts as a home run. Players advance only by being forced to the next base. For example, if a player is on first and the batter hits a double, the runners are on second and third. If a single follows then players are on first, second, and third. If the next batter hits a double, players are on second and third and two runs score.

Safety Considerations
Before hitting a ball, the batter should be sure that the fielders are ready.

Instructional Tips
If it is too easy to score runs, make the space between the cones smaller and move them farther from home plate. If it is too difficult to score runs, make the space between the cones larger and move them closer to home plate.

Cool-Down
This game works well as a cool-down.

60. Hot Box

Number of players	Experience	Playing area
Teams of 3	Experienced	Any flat field

Recommended Equipment
Two bases.

Setup
Put two bases 60 or 90 feet (18 or 27 meters) apart. A player stands on each base, one of them with a ball in hand. The third player stands midway between the two bases.

Key Objective
For the player in the middle (in the hot box) to get to one of the bases safely.

How to Play
The player with the ball moves forward to try to tag the player in the middle. The other base player moves closer to the player in the hot box. If the player in the hot box has an opportunity to run to the base by the player without the ball, she should do so. If the player in the hot box is getting too close to passing the base player without the ball, the base player with the ball throws the ball to the other base player. The base players try to squeeze the player in the hot box into a smaller and smaller area without letting her get by, and they eventually tag her. Players switch roles and see who can most often reach base safely.

Safety Considerations
Players may slide into a base. Make sure that the sliding area is safe and free from dangerous debris.

Instructional Tips
➤ Defensively, players should make as few throws as possible. They can fake throws and should run down the middle player when possible.

➤ The player in the middle should force as many throws as possible (hoping for an errant throw), fake direction to force a throw, and try to avoid a tag when being chased without leaving the base path.

Cool-Down
This activity is too vigorous to use as a cool-down.

61. Relay, Relay

Number of players	Experience	Playing area
2 or more teams of 3-8	Experienced	Any long, flat field

Recommended Equipment
One baseball per team, with each player holding a glove.

Setup
Each team lines up with players in a line five paces apart. The teams line up beside each other at least five paces apart.

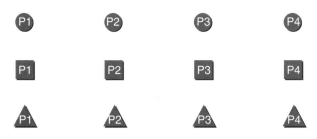

Key Objective
To pass a ball through the team as quickly as possible.

How to Play
On the signal to start, player 1 (P1) passes the ball to P2 (P1 then runs past the team and takes a position five paces past P4), who turns and passes to P3, who turns and passes to P4, who returns the pass to P3, who returns the pass to P2. The team repeats the cycle until P1 is at the head of the line and holding the ball.

Safety Considerations
Players need to keep their heads up so that they are always ready to receive a thrown ball.

Instructional Tips
The instructor can make the game more difficult by specifying the type of throw required and by increasing the distance between players. If players are far apart, they may need to hold their positions instead of running to the end of the line.

Cool-Down
This activity is too vigorous to use as a cool-down.

62. Right-Left Consecutive Bunt Pepper

Number of players	Experience	Playing area
Teams of 4	Experienced	Any flat field

Recommended Equipment
A bat, two balls, and three gloves.

Setup
One player (B) holds the bat, and a pitcher (P) stands 10 paces away at a pitcher's spot with a ball in hand. The other players, fielders 1 and 2 (F1 and F2), stand 5 paces to either side of the pitcher.

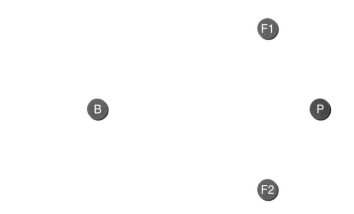

Key Objective
To bunt accurately as many times as possible in 10 pitches.

How to Play
The pitcher and F2 each have a ball. The pitcher pitches the ball. The batter bunts to the fielder on the batter's left. The pitcher goes to F2, and F2 goes to the pitcher's spot and pitches the ball. The batter bunts to the fielder on the batter's right. The pitcher goes to F1, and F1 goes to the pitcher's spot and pitches the ball. Play continues until the batter has received 10 pitches. Players rotate positions and repeat until all four players have batted 10 times. What was the total number of successful bunts?

Safety Considerations
Pitches should be slow, and batters should bunt softly.

Variations

➤ **Speed Pepper:** This variation is like Right-Left Consecutive Bunt Pepper, but players count how many successful bunts they can execute in 2 minutes. The pitcher must always pitch from the pitcher's spot.

➤ **Through-the-Infield Pepper:** This game is like Right-Left Consecutive Bunt Pepper, but the fielders back up five paces, the pitcher throws the ball at half speed, and the hitter hits the ball at half speed. The hitter tries to find an open spot between the fielders. Players count how many times they can hit safely in 40 attempts.

Cool-Down

This game works well as a cool-down if two additional fielders are added to slow the action.

CHAPTER 8

BASKETBALL

63. Throw to a Wall Relay

Number of players	Experience	Playing area
Teams of 3	All	Any flat surface with a wall

Recommended Equipment
One basketball per team.

Setup
Mark a restraining line five paces from a wall. The three players stand behind the line, and one player holds a basketball.

Key Objective
To see how many times the three players can each throw the ball against the wall in 2 minutes.

How to Play
The first player in line throws the ball against the wall. The second player in line catches the ball and from behind the restraining line throws the ball against the wall (the player may move in front of the restraining line to retrieve the ball but must throw the ball from behind it). The third player does the same, and then the three players repeat the sequence. They count how many cycles they can complete in 2 minutes.

Safety Considerations
Make sure that teams are far enough apart so that they do not inadvertently hit players from other teams who may be retrieving a misplaced ball.

Instructional Tips
Accuracy is more important than speed. The instructor can prescribe a certain throw—chest pass, bounce pass, overhead pass, or baseball pass—and may define a good throw as being one caught in the air or after only one bounce.

Variations

➤ **Triple Pass Wall Relay:** This variation is the same as Throw to a Wall Relay except that each player performs three consecutive passes to herself before the next player gets the ball.

➤ **Kick to a Wall Relay:** This variation is the same as Throw to a Wall Relay except that players use a soccer ball and kick it instead of throw it.

Cool-Down

This game works well as a cool-down, especially with a shorter distance to the wall and additional players on each team.

64. Pass Around

Number of players	Experience	Playing area
Groups of 2	All	Any flat surface to sit on

Recommended Equipment
One basketball for two players.

Setup
Two players sit tall on the floor back to back with their legs flat on the floor. One player holds a basketball.

Key Objective
To pass the ball quickly 30 times in both directions.

How to Play
At the signal to start, the player with the ball passes the ball to the right to her partner. The partner passes the ball to the right back to her, completing one pass each. The players continue to pass the ball in a circle 25 times (both players audibly count their passes). When the players have each completed 25 passes they change direction and pass the ball to the left 25 times. The group who completes 50 passes first is the winner.

Safety Considerations
Players should turn from the waist. If performing the turning action hurts, players should stop.

Variations
- ➤ **Standing Pass Around:** This variation is the same as Pass Around except that players stand back to back.
- ➤ **Up-and-Down Pass Around:** This game is like Pass Around except that players alternately perform 5 passes standing up and 5 passes sitting down. They repeat until they have completed 50 passes.

Cool-Down
This activity is too vigorous to be a cool-down.

65. Star Pass

Number of players	Experience	Playing area
Groups of 5	All	Any flat surface

Recommended Equipment
One ball per group to start with balls added until all players have one.

Setup
Five players stand in a circle approximately three to four steps in diameter. One player holds a ball.

Key Objective
To pass the ball without dropping it.

How to Play
The player with the ball passes the ball to the second player to her right. That player in turn passes the ball to the second player to his right. After five passes the ball should be back to the first player. When players understand the pattern, add a second ball, then a third, then a fourth, and finally a fifth ball.

Safety Considerations
Players must make sure that the player they are passing to knows the ball is coming, that they do not throw the ball too hard, and that they do not throw at a player's head.

Instructional Tips
When there are only one or two balls, the leader may want to specify the type of pass used (chest pass, bounce pass). When the group has three or more balls they should begin to synchronize their throws (all players throw the ball at the same time). Players need to communicate with each other the type of pass they are using and height and trajectory of their pass so that balls do not collide. When the group has three or more balls the leader may want to have players add an activity between throws, such as bouncing the ball once, making a fake pass to the left, and then making a pass. Alternatively, players could swing the ball once around their backs, make a fake pass to the left, and then make a pass. Everyone could swing the ball once

between their legs in a figure-8 motion, make a fake pass to the left, and then make a pass. Of course, many other variations are possible. For this activity to be successful, the group must remain in sync.

Variation

Mass Star Pass: Increase the number of players (but always keep an odd number). With five players the passer throws the ball to the second player to her right. With seven players the passer throws the ball to the third player to her right. With nine players the passer throws the ball to the fourth player to her right, and so on.

Cool-Down

This activity works great as a cool-down, especially with fewer balls, unless the group is proficient at executing with many balls.

66. Dribble Tag

Number of players	Experience	Playing area
Any number	Experienced	Any flat surface

Recommended Equipment
One basketball per player and one pool noodle for the it.

Setup
Place all players inside a defined area (half a basketball court or larger if there are more players).

Key Objective
For the it to tag another player.

How to Play
Assign one player to be it. At the signal to start, everyone dribbles a ball in the designated area (including the it), and the it tries to tag another player with a pool noodle she is holding in her other hand. When a player is tagged he gets the pool noodle and tries to tag another player, and the previous it gets the ball. If a player being chased loses her ball she becomes the next it.

Safety Considerations
The it can tag players only between the shoulders and waist.

Instructional Tips
For more running, the instructor can designate several its.

Variation
Dribble Tag the Ball: All players bounce a basketball, and the it tries to touch another player's ball. When the it is successful, the player whose ball was tagged becomes the new it.

Cool-Down
This game works well as a cool-down, especially with only one it.

67. Shoot for the Stars

Number of players	Experience	Playing area
1 player at a time	Experienced	Basketball hoop with a key

Recommended Equipment
One basketball per player.

Setup
A player begins at the foul line holding a basketball.

Key Objective
To hit four shots within 1 minute.

How to Play
At the signal to start, the player dribbles to the basket and does a layup. If the shot is successful she goes to the foul line and takes a shot. She then goes to the three-point line and finally to center court (or a line five paces back from the three-point line). If she misses a shot she must get her own rebound and take the shot again until she is successful before advancing to the next level. For younger players, adjust the lines so they are closer to the basket.

Variation
Sure Shot for the Stars: This variation is like Shoot for the Stars except that a layup is worth 1 point, a foul shot is worth 3 points, a "three-point" shot is worth 6 points, and a shot from center court is worth 20 points. The shooter can take any shot he wishes and can repeat the shot as often as he likes. The shooter retrieves all of his rebounds. The shooter scores as many points as he can within 1 minute.

Cool-Down
For an effective cool-down, players take two shots from each spot and add up their scores, but they are under no time limit.

68. Rebounding Trios

Number of players	Experience	Playing area
3 teams of 3	Experienced	An area with a basketball hoop

Recommended Equipment
One basketball per game.

Setup
One group of three (team A) stands outside the three-point line with one player holding a basketball. A second group of three (team B) stands outside the key. The third group of three (team C) stands inside the key.

Key Objective
To be the first team to score 15 points.

How to Play
A player from team A takes a shot from behind the three-point line. If successful his team scores 1 point, and a different member of team A takes a three-point shot. This sequence continues until someone from team A misses a shot. The objective for the players on team B and team C is to get the rebound. After a team A player takes a shot, team B players can penetrate the key in an effort to secure the rebound. If a team C player secures the rebound, team C scores 1 point. If a team

B player secures the rebound, team B scores 1 point. Following the rebound the teams rotate. Team C goes outside the three-point line and takes the place of team A, team A takes the place of team B, and team B goes inside the key to take the place of team C.

Safety Considerations
No rough play outside the rules of basketball is permitted.

Instructional Tips
This game is an excellent warm-up that emphasizes positional play.

Variations
- ➤ **Rebounding Doubles:** This variation is like Rebounding Triples except that each team consists of two players.
- ➤ **Two Rebounding Trios:** Eliminate team B. Team C stands near the basket to get the rebound. Team A stands behind the three-point line. A player on team A takes a shot. If the shot is successful, team A scores 1 point, and another player on team A takes a shot. After a player shoots, team A players can cross the three-point line. If the shot misses, the team that secures the rebound scores 1 point and becomes (or remains) the shooting team.
- ➤ **Two Rebounding Doubles:** This game is like Two Rebounding Trios except that each team consists of two players.

Cool-Down
This game is probably a little too vigorous to serve as a cool-down.

69. Professional Bump

Number of players	Experience	Playing area
5 to 50	Experienced	A basketball court with several baskets marked with free-throw lines

Recommended Equipment

Two basketballs per basket.

Setup

Have all the players stand in a line behind each other, with the first player standing at the free-throw line (or other designated spot) at one of the baskets. (If you have many players, position groups of players at every other basket or every basket if necessary.) The first two players each hold a basketball.

Key Objective

To advance to as many baskets as possible by "bumping" up from other players.

How to Play

The first player takes a foul shot. If the shooter is successful she retrieves the ball, passes it to the next player in line, and goes to the back of the line. If the shooter misses she retrieves the ball and keeps shooting until the ball goes in. Meanwhile, the next player in line begins shooting. If he scores a basket before the first player does, he moves to the next basket. The game continues for 5 minutes, and players see how many baskets they can move up.

Safety Considerations

Players must be careful when retrieving balls so that they do not crash into the other shooter.

Instructional Tips

Although shooters need to shoot quickly, they benefit from taking focused shots rather than wild throws.

Variation

Elimination Bump: This game is like Professional Bump except that a player who does not score a basket before the player behind him does is eliminated from the game.

Cool-Down

This game works well as a cool-down. If Elimination Bump is played, those eliminated often linger and walk around to see who will win before leaving the gym.

70. Take-a-Break Keep-Away

Number of players	Experience	Playing area
2 teams of 3-6	Experienced	Any flat surface

Recommended Equipment
One basketball per game.

Setup
Define a playing area, something like a badminton court or half a volleyball court. Both teams are on the court, and one of the teams has a ball.

Key Objective
To make 10 consecutive passes to score 1 point.

How to Play
Players attempt to pass the ball to their teammates by throwing it. Handing the ball to a teammate is not permitted. Every set of 10 consecutive passes counts for 1 point. To win the game, teams must score 5 points. The player with the ball can only pivot on one foot and may not dribble or travel. The defending team tries to intercept the passes. If the defending team intercepts a pass or a pass goes out of bounds, the defending team gets the ball and attempts to make 10 consecutive passes. The player who made the last bad pass takes a break by sitting on the floor until her team gets the ball again. This rule gives a slight advantage to the offensive team.

Safety Considerations
Players should keep their heads up to avoid crashing into each other. No body contact is permitted.

Instructional Tips
Players need to find open spaces so that their teammates can pass them the ball.

Variations

➤ **Specific Pass Take-a-Break Keep-Away:** This variation is like Take-a-Break Keep-Away except that players may use only one type of pass, for example, a bounce pass or chest pass.

➤ **Multisport Take-a-Break Keep-Away:** This game is like Take-a-Break Keep-Away, but players use different sport passes and balls.

Cool-Down

This activity works well as a cool-down if the playing area is not too large.

CHAPTER 9

FOOTBALL

71. Hot Football

Number of players	Experience	Playing area
Groups of 7-15	All	Any flat surface

Recommended Equipment
One football per group.

Setup
Players stand in a circle, and one player holds a football.

Key Objective
To see how long the group can successfully pass the football.

How to Play
At the signal to start, the player with the ball passes it to someone not immediately beside her. The player receiving the football has a half second to hold the ball and pass it to another player not immediately beside him. Play continues until someone drops the ball, holds it for more than a half second, or passes it to someone immediately beside her. Measure the time until the infraction occurred. Players repeat the game and try to better their previous best time.

Variations
> **Name Calling Hot Football:** When a player catches the ball he calls out his name. This game helps players learn each other's names at the beginning of the season.

> **Double Name Calling Hot Football:** When a player catches the ball she calls out her name, and when she passes it she calls out the name of the player she is throwing the ball to.

> **Hot Footballs:** This variation is like Hot Football except that the group uses two or more balls at the same time. Groups can also use two or more balls when playing Name Calling or Double Name Calling.

- ➤ **Rotating Hot Football:** This game is like Hot Football except that players walk around in a circle while they play the game. Players can also move in a circle while playing the other variations.
- ➤ **Multisport Hot Ball or Puck:** Any of the variations can be played using other sports equipment and passes.

Cool-Down

This activity works well as a cool-down when players walk and use a limited number of balls.

72. Wild Flags

Number of players	Experience	Playing area
Any number	All	Any flat surface

Recommended Equipment
A pair of football flags per player.

Setup
Designate an area (for example, a square 10 paces across for 10 players or 20 paces across for 20 players). Position players inside the square.

Key Objective
To gain the most flags in a specified time.

How to Play
All players are it and must always have two flags hanging from belts around their waists. Players try to grab each other's flags. Players may not cover their flags with their hands. If a player grabs a flag but has lost one or both of his flags, he must replace the lost flag with the new flag. Players who have both of their flags continue to try to grab other flags. They hold the extra flags in one of their hands. Play continues for a specified time.

Instructional Tips
Players will quickly realize that they need to be aware of their spatial relationship with other players.

Variation
Wild Clothespins: This variation is like Wild Flags except that clothespins are used instead of flags. Players attach two clothespins to their shirts, one on either side. When players gain another clothespin, they place it on their shirts.

Cool-Down
This game can be a fun cool-down.

73. Round the Corners Snap

Number of players	Experience	Playing area
Groups of 3	All	Any flat surface

Recommended Equipment
One football and four cones for each group.

Setup
Position four cones in a square, four to six paces apart. Players stand as shown in the figure.

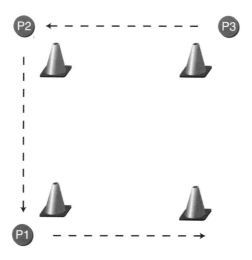

Key Objective
To see how many successful snaps can be accomplished in 2 to 3 minutes.

How to Play
At the signal to begin, player 1 (P1) snaps the ball to P2. P1 then runs forward past the other cone. P2 then snaps the ball to P3 and runs forward to the position vacated by P1. P3 then snaps the ball to P1 and runs forward to the position vacated by P2. They continue until the time is up.

Variations

➤ **Round the Corners Lateral:** This variation is the same as Round the Corners Snap except that players use a sidearm lateral pass.

➤ **Round the Corners Multisport Passes:** This game is like Round the Corners Snap except that players perform a pass that they would use in basketball, soccer, hockey, or volleyball.

Cool-Down

This game works well as a cool-down if players reduce their speed and measure success by the number of completed passes with no time limit to beat.

74. Completed Passes

Number of players	Experience	Playing area
Teams of 6-12	Experienced	Any flat field

Recommended Equipment
Four footballs per group.

Setup
Two quarterbacks line up opposite each other 20 paces apart. Two or more receivers line up 10 paces to the right of each quarterback.

Key Objective
To make as many consecutive catches as possible.

How to Play
Receiver 1 (R1) runs a pattern, and quarterback 1 (QB1) throws a pass to him. At the same time, R2 runs a similar pattern the opposite way and QB2 throws a pass to her. After catching the ball each receiver puts the ball at the feet of the other quarterback and goes to the back of the opposite line. R3 and R4 run and catch. They repeat and count how many consecutive catches they make.

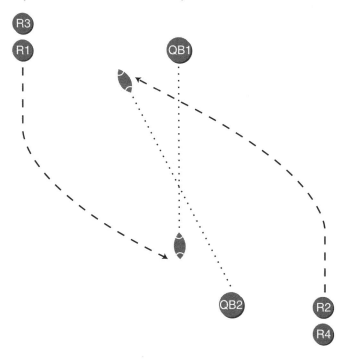

Safety Considerations

Players should be aware of where they are and where their team-mates are so that they do not run into each other when running their pass patterns.

Instructional Tips

Players should use various patterns.

Cool-Down

This game works well as a cool-down, especially if there are a few more players and they run pass patterns at three-quarter speed.

75. Ultimate Football

Number of players	Experience	Playing area
2 teams of 4-12	Experienced	Any flat field

Recommended Equipment
One football per game.

Setup
The field should be approximately 20 paces wide and 40 paces long with a goal area 10 paces deep behind each goal area. The two teams line up on their goal lines, and one team has the ball.

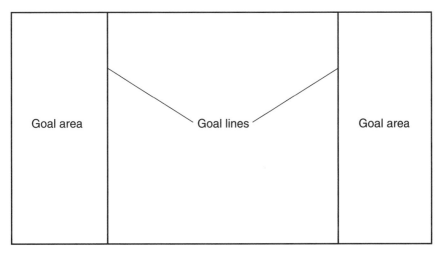

Goal area   Goal lines   Goal area

Key Objective
To score more points than the other team scores by catching the ball in the other team's goal area.

How to Play
On the signal to begin, players from both teams move onto the field of play. The player with the ball may not run or walk with the ball and must pass it to a teammate within 3 seconds of receiving it. Any type of pass is allowed, or a leader can specify that players only use certain passes. A player defending the passer must be at least three paces away.

If the ball is intercepted the other team passes the ball toward their opponent's goal area. If the pass is incomplete the other team picks up the ball and attempts to pass it toward their opponent's goal area. If a team catches the ball in their opponent's goal area, they score a point. When a team scores both teams get behind their goal lines and go on the field after the signal to resume play.

Instructional Tips
With fewer players, make the field smaller.

Variation
Ultimate Soccer (or Hockey or Lacrosse): This variation is like Ultimate Football except that players use a soccer ball that they kick and trap, or hockey sticks and a puck that they pass and trap, or sticks and a ball that they pass and catch.

Cool-Down
This game can serve as a cool-down if the playing area is reduced in size.

CHAPTER 10

HOCKEY

76. Obstacle Course for Hockey

Number of players	Experience	Playing area
Teams of 3	All	Ice surface

Recommended Equipment
Cones.

Setup
Design an obstacle course.

Key Objective
For teams of three players to complete the course as quickly as possible.

How to Play
Be creative and set up an obstacle course. The course can include skating around cones, sliding underneath a hockey stick balanced atop two cones, jumping over a hockey stick balanced atop two cones, shooting a puck into a goal, and skating a specific distance.

Safety Considerations
Be sure that any obstacles are far enough away from the boards that players will not hurt themselves should they fall at some point in the course.

Instructional Tips
➤ Obstacle courses can be competitive, fun warm-up experiences. To maximize activity, have the second player begin when the first player reaches a predetermined spot in the course.
➤ Let the players have some fun by taking turns in developing a different obstacle course for each practice.

Variation
Multisport Obstacle Course: Design an obstacle course similar to the Obstacle Course for Hockey but make it applicable to another sport.

Cool-Down
An obstacle course tends to be too vigorous to use as a cool-down.

77. Hockey Soccer

Number of players	Experience	Playing area
Teams of 3-5	Experienced	Ice surface

Recommended Equipment
One soccer ball (or puck) and four cones per game.

Setup
Set up two goals 2 yards or 2 meters wide at the boards on either side of a rink played across the width. Sidelines could be the end of the rink to the blue line and between the blue lines. One team has the ball near their goal.

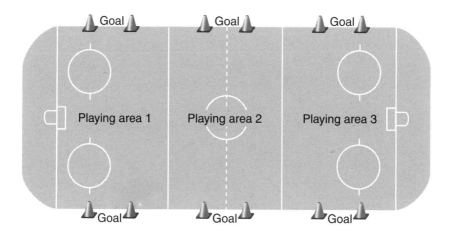

Key Objective
Players score goals by kicking the ball into the opponent's goal.

How to Play
Each team tries to gain possession of the ball, kick the ball to pass it to teammates, and score by kicking the ball into the goal. Players may not use their arms or hands to contact the ball. If that occurs the other team gets the ball at that point, and a player can kick the ball once without being defended. Players should wear ice skates.

Variation

Puck Soccer: This variation is the same as Hockey Soccer except that players use a puck as the object to kick rather than a soccer ball. The small puck is much more difficult to kick.

Cool-Down

With a few more players added to each team to minimize movement, this game works well as a cool-down.

78. Puck Handle Score!

Number of players	Experience	Playing area
Groups of 5-10	Experienced	Ice surface

Recommended Equipment
A hockey stick and puck for each player and six cones.

Setup
Set up cones and players as shown.

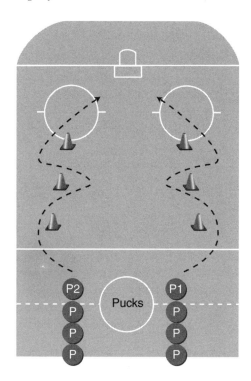

Key Objective
To score as many goals as possible in 10 shots.

How to Play
The first player (P1) starts with a puck at center, skates around the outside of the first cone on the right, weaves through the other two cones, and takes a shot on goal as soon as she is past the third cone.

The next player (P2) does the same but starts by going to the first cone on the left. After a player has taken a shot he retrieves his puck, skates back to the center of the rink, and does the challenge again going to the alternate side. Players go five times to each side. The player who scores the most goals out of 10 shots is the winner.

Safety Considerations
When retrieving their pucks, players must be careful that they avoid being hit by the next shot. When they are returning to center they must not skate into a player skating through the cones.

Cool-Down
This game works well as a cool-down.

79. 3-on-2 Keep-Away

Number of players	Experience	Playing area
Groups of 5-10	Experienced	Ice surface

Recommended Equipment
A hockey stick for each player and two pucks for each group.

Setup
A team of three goes inside the face-off circle and has the puck. A team of two waits outside the circle. (For older players this game works better with two players inside the circle and just one player outside the circle.)

Key Objective
For the team of three to keep the puck away from the team of two as long as possible.

How to Play
A team of two goes inside the face-off circle and tries to knock the puck away from the team of three. When the team of three loses the puck (the puck goes outside the circle or the team of two takes the puck away), one player of the team of three stays in the circle and the other two leave the circle and retrieve the puck. The team of two becomes a team of three and has the puck. A new team of two that was waiting outside the face-off circle now comes in and tries to get the puck from the new team of three.

Instructional Tips
Players can protect the puck more effectively by keeping their bodies between the puck and their opponents.

Cool-Down
This game works well as a cool-down.

80. Two-Line Pass

Number of players	Experience	Playing area
Groups of 5-10	Experienced	Ice surface

Recommended Equipment

A hockey stick for each player and two to five pucks for each team.

Setup

Divide players into two teams. Have each team divide into two groups and take positions in the zones as indicated.

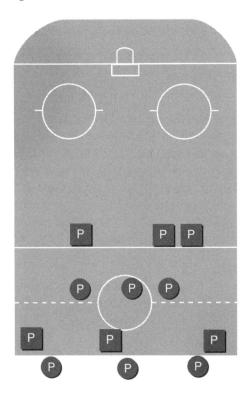

Key Objective

For the players between the blue lines to get the puck as many times as possible within the preset time limit (2 minutes).

How to Play

At the signal to start, players behind their blue line attempt to pass the puck to one of their players on the other side of the center line. If a player successfully receives the pass, his team scores 1 point. If a player between the blue lines successfully intercepts a pass, her team scores 1 point. When players receive or intercept a pass and the point is awarded, the puck is given to the opposing team behind their blue line.

Variation

Lane Two-Line Pass: Divide the rink lengthwise into two or three lanes with the use of cones. This game is like Two-Line Pass except that it is played in a narrower area.

Cool-Down

This game works great as a cool-down, but the leader may wish to reduce the number of pucks.

81. Double-Up

Number of players	Experience	Playing area
2 teams of 3-8	Experienced	Ice surface

Recommended Equipment
A hockey stick for each player and one puck for each team.

Setup
Players skate in a circle (around the two face-off circles or around the two face-off circles and the goal). Players from the same team are always separated from each other by a player from the other team.

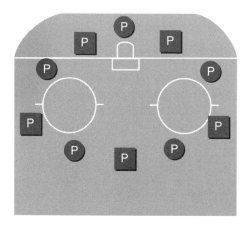

Key Objective
To pass the pucks, while skating around in a circle, so that one team's puck passes the other team's puck.

How to Play
Two players on opposite sides of the circle (or otherwise defined skating area) each have a puck. Everyone starts skating in the same direction at a moderate speed. On a signal to begin, the pucks are passed forward to the next teammate. The receiver controls the puck and passes it to the next teammate. Players continue to pass the puck forward. Players attempt to pass the puck as quickly as possible in an attempt to pass the other team's puck. If a puck passes the other

team's puck, the passing team scores a point. Players then switch skating directions. After the two pucks are placed at opposite sides of the skating area, the game is played again.

Cool-Down

This activity works well as a cool-down if players slow the speed of skating.

CHAPTER 11

SOCCER

82. Crazy Eights

Number of players	Experience	Playing area
Any number	All	Any flat surface

Recommended Equipment
One soccer ball per player and two cones.

Setup
Set up two cones five paces apart (farther apart if there are many players).

Key Objective
To complete 10 laps of the course successfully.

How to Play
All players begin behind one of the cones, each with a soccer ball at her feet. At the signal to begin, they all dribble through a figure-8 pattern around the cones. The more players and the closer together the cones, the more congested the middle is between the two cones. Each player tries to complete 10 laps of the course. Dribbling around both cones is considered 1 lap.

Safety Considerations
No running or deliberate body contact is permitted. Players should keep their heads up, especially when they are going through the mob in the middle.

Instructional Tips
Players should work on controlling the ball by keeping it close to their feet.

Variation
Multisport Crazy Eights: This drill can work for other sports such as basketball, lacrosse, and hockey.

Cool-Down
This activity works great as a cool-down, particularly if the cones are not too far apart and movement is limited to a quick walk.

83. Pit Ball Terror

Number of players	Experience	Playing area
2 teams of 3-5	All	Any flat surface

Recommended Equipment
One or two soccer balls per game and one cone.

Setup
Mark out a circle approximately 10 to 15 paces in diameter (the center circle might work but may be too large). Place a cone in the middle of the circle. All players are outside the circle.

Key Objective
To kick the ball against the cone.

How to Play
All players are situated outside the circle. One team starts with the ball and attempts to score by kicking the ball to hit the cone. The other team tries to prevent a score. If they gain possession of the ball they try to score. Players may not go into the circle unless the ball stops inside the circle. When that happens a defensive player can go in and have a free kick to a player outside the circle. If a player goes into the circle to retrieve a moving ball, the other team gets a free kick from that spot at the cone. The free kick is almost certain to be a goal so players should not go inside the circle.

Instructional Tips
Players need to create space for themselves when they do not have the ball so that they can receive a pass and advance a scoring possibility.

Cool-Down
This game works well as a cool-down.

84. Throw-In Ball

Number of players	Experience	Playing area
2 teams of 3-9	All	Any flat surface

Recommended Equipment
One soccer ball per game and four cones.

Setup
Set up two goals by placing cones approximately 8 paces apart (3 imaginary paces high). The goals should be 30 paces apart.

Key Objective
To score a goal by using a proper throw-in.

How to Play
Both teams line up on their own goal lines, with one team holding the ball. At the signal to begin, the offensive team moves onto the playing field to receive a pass while the defending team moves onto the field to intercept the pass. The player with the ball does a legal throw-in (without the run) and passes the ball to a teammate who catches the ball with his hands. If the pass is incomplete the other team gets the ball where they pick the ball up. If the pass is complete the new player with the ball does a throw-in to another teammate in an effort to take the ball down the field and score a goal (a throw-in that goes into the goal). A player has 3 seconds to pass the ball. A player defending against the throw-in cannot be closer than three paces. When a goal is scored both teams line up on their respective goal lines. The team who was scored on begins play from their goal line.

Instructional Tips
This game emphasizes proper throw-ins.

Cool-Down
This game is an excellent way to cool down.

85. Split Triangle Run

Number of players	Experience	Playing area
Teams of 3	All	Any flat surface

Recommended Equipment
One soccer ball per group.

Setup
Three players stand in a triangle formation approximately five paces apart. Player 1 (P1) has a soccer ball.

Key Objective
To complete one lap of the field (or more if desired).

How to Play
P1 passes the ball to P2 and then runs between P2 and P3. P2 passes the ball to P3 and then runs between P3 and P1. P3 passes the ball to P1 and then runs between P1 and P2. They repeat the sequence until the group has traveled once around the field.

Safety Considerations
Players need to be careful not to run into soccer posts, playing benches, or other objects around the playing field.

Instructional Tips
Players can never be farther than five paces from each other.

Variations
➤ **Throw-In Split Triangle Run:** This variation is similar to Split Triangle Run, but players use a free throw instead of a pass. Players should be around 10 paces apart for this activity. Receiving players should trap the ball, not catch it with their hands.

➤ **Multisport Split Triangle Run:** This drill can work for other sports such as basketball or lacrosse.

Cool-Down
This game works great as a cool-down if players use a slower pace.

86. Double Cone Ball

Number of players	Experience	Playing area
Pairs	All	Any flat surface

Recommended Equipment
One soccer ball per game and four cones.

Setup
Set up two cones 3 paces apart (like a goal). Another pair of cones should be 10 paces away.

Key Objective
To score more goals, by kicking the ball against one of the opponent's cones, than the opponent does.

How to Play
One player begins with the ball and attempts to dribble by her opponent and kick the ball against one of her opponent's cones. The other player tries to prevent her from doing so and tries to intercept the ball and kick it against one of her opponent's cones. After a player has scored a goal, the other player gets to dribble the ball three paces from her goal line before her opponent can defend against her.

Safety Considerations
No body checking is permitted.

Variation
Triple Cone Ball: This game is played the same way that Double Cone Ball is played, but three players play with six cones placed in a triangular configuration.

Cool-Down
This game is a fun cool-down activity.

87. One-Goal Soccer

Number of players	Experience	Playing area
Teams of 2-8	All	Any flat surface

Recommended Equipment
One soccer ball per game and two cones.

Setup
Set up two cones three paces apart (like a goal).

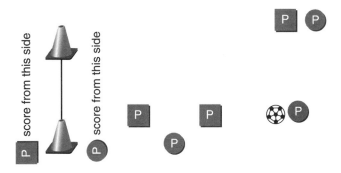

Key Objective
To score more goals, by kicking the ball through the opponent's goal, than the opponent does.

How to Play
One team begins with the ball and attempts to dribble and pass by the opposing team and kick into the goal, between the two cones. The other team tries to prevent a goal and tries to intercept the ball and score their own goal. For the other team to score a goal they must first pass or dribble the ball to the other side of the goal. After a team has scored a goal, the team scored against gets to dribble the ball three paces from their goal before the other team can defend against them.

Safety Considerations
No body checking is permitted.

Cool-Down
This game is a fun cool-down activity.

88. Dribble Goal Line

Number of players	Experience	Playing area
Teams of 3	Experienced	Any flat surface

Recommended Equipment
One soccer ball and cones to delineate a field.

Setup
Define four corners for a field with two sidelines and two goal lines. Players line up on their respective goal lines to start play. One team is given a ball.

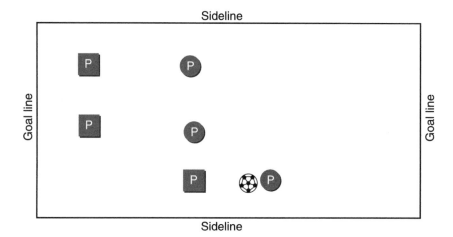

Key Objective
To score goals by dribbling or trapping a ball just over the opponent's goal line.

How to Play
The players with the ball dribble and pass the ball to each other. They attempt to dribble the ball over their opponent's goal line or pass it to a teammate who is able to trap the ball just over (less than three paces) the line for a goal. When a team scores a goal, the other team gets to dribble the ball freely for three paces past their goal line before being defended against. If a ball goes out of bounds, the team that did not touch it last gets to throw or roll the ball into play.

Safety Considerations

If this game is played indoors make sure that there is adequate room between the goal line and the wall so that no one runs into the wall.

Instructional Tips

This game allows players to practice shielding, dribbling, and passing.

Cool-Down

This game works well as a cool-down.

89. Grid Pass

Number of players	Experience	Playing area
Groups of 4	Experienced	Any flat surface

Recommended Equipment
One soccer ball and cones to delineate a grid.

Setup
Define a square grid with sides approximately four to six paces long. Three players stand on corners of the grid, and one player stands in the middle.

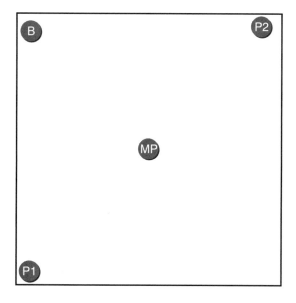

Key Objective
The players on the outside must pass the ball to a partner on an adjacent corner without having the ball intercepted or without being tagged while holding the ball.

How to Play
One player (player B) begins with the ball in one of the grid corners. The other two players (P1 and P2) are positioned at adjacent corners, leaving one corner open. The player with the ball can pass it only to

one of the two adjacent corners (he cannot pass the ball across the grid or dribble the ball). Once the pass has been made, the player who did not receive it moves to the open corner to give the receiver two corners to pass the ball to. The middle player (MP) tries to intercept the ball or force a bad pass. Play continues until a player makes a bad pass or the player in the middle intercepts the ball. When that happens the player who made the errant pass goes into the middle and is replaced by the MP.

Instructional Tips

This game helps players learn to execute short, accurate passes. Players should use deception and not telegraph whom they intend to pass the ball to. Players without the ball should always ensure the possibility of two receivers.

Variation

Multisport Grid Pass: Grid Pass can also be done with basketball, lacrosse, or even overhead or underhand passes in volleyball.

Cool-Down

This game works well as a cool-down, especially if the grid is a little smaller.

90. 2-4 Keep-Away

Number of players	Experience	Playing area
2 teams of 3-4	Experienced	Any flat surface

Recommended Equipment
One soccer ball per group and six cones.

Setup
Use six cones to define two adjacent squares. Each square should be approximately 15 paces long (the smaller the square, the more difficult it is to successfully pass the ball). The offensive team has the ball, and all their players are in one square. The defensive team has two players in each square.

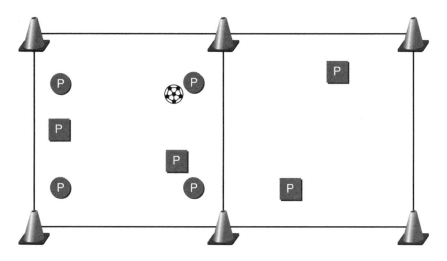

Key Objective
For the team with the ball to make 10 consecutive passes to score 1 point.

How to Play
Players attempt to pass the ball to their teammates by kicking the ball. Handing the ball to a teammate is not permitted. A team scores 1 point by making 10 consecutive passes. To win a game, a team must score 5 points. The defending team tries to intercept the passes. If the defending team intercepts a pass or a pass goes out of bounds, the

defending team gets the ball on their side and attempts to make 10 consecutive passes. The two defensive players join their two teammates on their own court. The team that was on the offense is now on defense and sends two players into the other team's court to try to break up their passes.

Safety Considerations
Players should keep their heads up to avoid crashing into each other. Body contact is not permitted.

Instructional Tips
Players must find open spaces so that their teammates can pass them the ball.

Variations
➤ **Basketball Pass 2-4 Keep-Away:** This variation is the same as 2-4 Keep-Away except that players may only use a specific type of basketball pass, such as a bounce pass or chest pass.

➤ **Multisport 2-4 Keep-Away:** This game is the same as 2-4 Keep-Away except that players use lacrosse sticks and a lacrosse ball, a soccer ball, or other equipment.

Cool-Down
This game works well as a cool-down as long as the playing area is not too large.

91. Jugglers

Number of players	Experience	Playing area
1	Experienced	Open space

Recommended Equipment
One soccer ball for each player.

Setup
Each player has a ball in an open area.

Key Objective
To see how long each player can juggle the ball.

How to Play
A player drops a ball to her feet and kicks the ball back up to herself. She continues to keep the ball up as long as possible using any part of her body but her arms and hands. For beginning players, allow one bounce on the ground between kicks.

Safety Considerations
Before players begin juggling they should be at least a couple yards or meters away from other players or obstacles.

Instructional Tips
Kicking the ball with a bit of backspin helps the juggler keep the ball nearby.

Variation
Group Juggle: Instead of a single juggler, two to five jugglers can work together using one ball. The group tries to see how many successive kicks they can perform before the ball lands on the ground. Jugglers can kick the ball to themselves a maximum of three times before passing the ball to another juggler.

Cool-Down
This activity can work well as a cool-down.

92. Soccer Wallball

Number of players	Experience	Playing area
2	Experienced	An area with a wall

Recommended Equipment
One soccer ball per game.

Setup
Draw a square on a wall starting from the ground that is 2 yards or meters wide and high. Starting at the wall, draw a rectangle on the ground approximately 3 yards or meters from the wall. Add one more line on the wall, 1 foot or 20 centimeters above the ground. In the end you have a small racquetball court without the side or back walls.

Key Objective
Players try to make a legal kick against the wall that their opponent cannot return.

How to Play
Determine who will start the game by seeing who can juggle (kick) the ball to themselves the most consecutive times. The server stands behind the court, drops the ball, and off the bounce kicks the ball against the wall inside the lined area. The other player plays the ball in the air or lets it bounce a maximum of one time before returning a kicked ball against the wall inside the lined area. Play continues until one player is unable to return the ball against the wall inside the lined area. The other player then receives a point. The player receiving the point goes behind the court and starts play again by dropping the ball and kicking it against the wall. They play until one player scores 15 points.

Instructional Tips
Control of the ball is crucial to success in this game.

Cool-Down
This game works well as a cool-down.

93. Soccer Volleyball

Number of players	Experience	Playing area
2 teams of 4	Expert	Volleyball court

Recommended Equipment
One soccer ball per game and a volleyball net.

Setup
Each team distributes their players around the court as in volleyball.

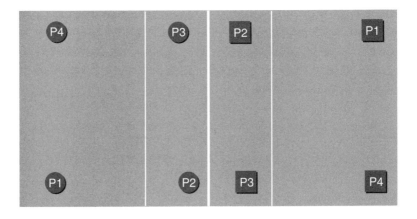

Key Objective
To score 25 points on the other team.

How to Play
Player 1 (P1) from one of the teams serves the ball by kicking it over the net (punt or drop kick) and into the opponent's court. A failed attempt results in a side out (the other team rotates all their players one position clockwise, gets a point, and serves the ball). The returning team can play the ball as many times as they wish but must get the ball over the net and into their opponent's court. Failure to do so results in a point and service for the other team. Players may contact the ball several times in a row. The ball may bounce once between players but not between consecutive hits by one player. Players may contact the ball and advance it with any part of the body except their arms and hands.

Safety Considerations

Be sure that volleyball posts are padded.

Instructional Tips

Control of the ball is crucial to success in this game.

Variations

➤ **Soccer Tennis:** This game is like Soccer Volleyball except that it is played on a tennis court (or a volleyball court with the net hung at tennis height) with two players per side.

➤ **One-Bounce Soccer Volleyball (Tennis):** For more skilled players, limit the number of bounces to one per side each time the ball goes over the net.

Cool-Down

This game works well as a cool-down with six players on a side in Soccer Volleyball and three players on a side in Soccer Tennis.

CHAPTER 12

VOLLEYBALL

94. Shower Volleyball

Number of players	Experience	Playing area
2 teams of 6 or more	Experienced	Volleyball court

Recommended Equipment
Volleyball court with a net and four volleyballs.

Setup
Place six or more players on either side of the net. Each team has two volleyballs.

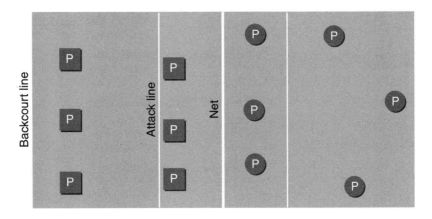

Key Objective
To score points by making the ball land on the opponent's court.

How to Play
At the signal to begin, players with a ball throw the ball (underhand) over the net into the opponent's court. Players on the other side try to catch the ball; if they fail and the ball lands in the court, the other team scores a point. If a player catches the ball, she can throw it to a teammate, with a maximum of two passes per side, or throw it back over the net. If the ball lands outside the court on a throw, the receiving side scores a point. Players may not hold the ball for longer than 3 seconds. Players may not hit the ball with any part of the body, but they can hit another ball with a ball they happen to be holding. That action does not count as a pass or throw. The teams play until one team reaches 25 points.

Safety Considerations

Encourage students to be aware of each other (keeping their heads up and calling the balls they are going for) so that they do not bump into each other.

Instructional Tips

Remind students to spread themselves out on defense to fill the court and to look for the open areas on offense to score.

Variations

➤ **Mass-Ball Shower Volleyball:** To add to the confusion and fun, use six or more balls. Scoring will go more quickly with more balls.

➤ **No-Pass Shower Volleyball:** Passes are not permitted. All caught balls must be thrown back over the net.

➤ **I Spy Shower Volleyball:** Each team sends one of their teammates into the opponent's court. If that player catches the ball, his team scores a point in addition to the usual point scoring. To prevent rough play, no body contact is permitted in this game.

Cool-Down

This game works wonderfully as a cool-down activity.

95. Balloon Volleyball

Number of players	Experience	Playing area
12 or more	Experienced	Volleyball court

Recommended Equipment
Volleyball court with a net and one balloon per player.

Setup
Place players on the court (from the net to the attack line, which is the back line in this game) as indicated and give each player an inflated balloon.

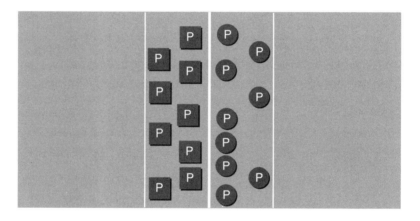

Key Objective
To get as many balloons as possible to land on the floor inside the opponent's court within 2 minutes.

How to Play
At the signal to begin, all players hit the balloons with any part of their bodies in an effort to get the balloons over the net. If a balloon hits the ground inside a team's court, the other team scores a point. If a balloon hits the ground outside a defending team's court, the defending team scores a point.

Safety Considerations
To prevent ankle injuries, do not allow students to jump. Be sure that posts are properly padded.

Instructional Tips
Have a few extra balloons on hand in case some break.

Variation
Short Balloon Volleyball: This game is played the same way as Balloon Volleyball is played, but only one or two players are on each side and they use only one balloon. Service can be delivered from anywhere in the small court but must be hit up (no spike serves).

Cool-Down
Limit the number of balloons to one or two for each four players to reduce the activity level.

96. Volleyball Relay

Number of players	Experience	Playing area
Teams of 4 or more	Experienced	Volleyball court

Recommended Equipment
Volleyball court with a net and one volleyball per team.

Setup
Place players on the court as shown. Give player 1 (P1) on each team a volleyball.

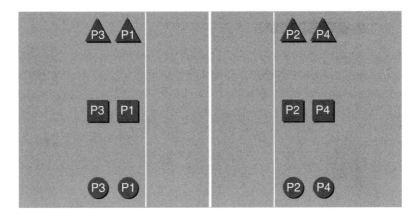

Key Objective
To see how many successful rotations a team can make.

How to Play
At the signal to begin, player 1 from each team passes the ball (set or forearm pass) to player 2 behind the attack line, who then passes the ball back over the net to player 3, and so on. After players set the ball they move forward and touch the net, and then move behind the attack line to make their next pass. Play continues for a team until their ball is not successfully passed over the net. Count how many times each team consecutively goes through the complete rotation. Players try again following an errant pass.

Safety Considerations
Be sure that posts are properly padded.

Instructional Tips

Teachers may need to watch for illegal passes (carrying the ball or double hitting the ball). Players should use different passes. They can start with any hit, then use just overhead passes, and finally use just forearm passes.

Variations

- ➤ **Running Volleyball Relay:** This game is like Volleyball Relay except that a cone is placed three to six paces behind the attack line. Each time a player sets the ball the setter must run around the cone and then get ready to make the next pass.

- ➤ **Long-Ball Volleyball Relay:** Choose a line four to five paces in front of the backcourt line. Players must take all passes between the backcourt line and the line four to five paces from the backcourt line. Any pass taken from outside this area is considered a fault, and play is stopped. Count the successful rotations and have players try again.

Cool-Down

Increase the number of players per team to reduce the amount of running and the vigor of the activity.

ₛetting Threes

Number of players	Experience	Playing area
Groups of 3	Experienced	Volleyball court

Recommended Equipment
Volleyball court and one volleyball.

Setup
Position players as shown. Player 1 (P1) holds the ball.

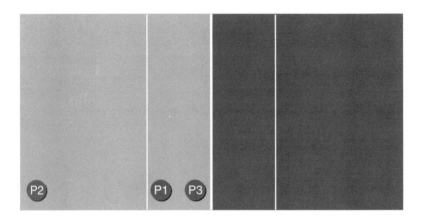

Key Objective
To count how many consecutive overhead passes three teammates can complete in 2 minutes.

How to Play
P1 passes the ball toward P2, who runs forward and sets the ball to P3 at the position P1 vacated. After P1 passes the ball she runs to the end line, touches it, turns, and gets ready to receive the pass from P3. After P2 passes the ball he runs to the net, touches it, turns, and gets ready to receive the pass from P1 again. Players continue to pass the ball, run to the end line or net, turn, and face the passer to receive the pass and make a pass.

Instructional Tips

The higher the sets, the more time players have to get ready to receive and pass the ball and not break their consecutive passing streak. Lower sets, however, allow players to complete more passes.

Variation

Forearm Threes: Players pass all balls using only forearm passes.

Cool-Down

This game can work well as a cool-down by adding two players (for a total of five) and requiring each team to complete a specified number of consecutive passes (100 or 150 passes).

ꓼ0zen Tag

Number of players	Experience	Playing area
Groups of 6 or more	Experienced	Volleyball court

Recommended Equipment
Volleyball court.

Setup
Place players on the court in a scattered formation and identify one player as being it.

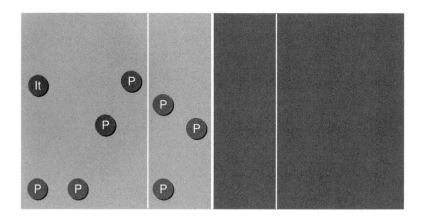

Key Objective
For the it to freeze all the players.

How to Play
At the signal to begin, the it tries to tag the other players. When a player is tagged she stands with her feet spread at least shoulder-width apart. If another player can dive between her legs the frozen player is free again. When a player steps outside the boundary he is frozen until the end of the game because no other player can go outside the boundaries to thaw the player out. If the it freezes everyone, the first player frozen becomes the new it.

Safety Considerations

This game works better if players have been taught how to dive in volleyball. If a net is up be sure that posts are properly padded. You may want to give the its a pool noodle or foam tube to tag players with so that no one is inadvertently pushed over while being tagged.

Instructional Tips

If the it finds it too difficult to freeze everyone, appoint a second it.

Variations

➤ **Frozen Ball Tag:** This game is the same as Frozen Tag except that the it freezes a player by gently throwing a ball against her. If you suspect that the throws will be too hard, have the it throw with the nondominant hand.

➤ **Soccer Frozen Tag:** This game is played the same way that Frozen Tag is played except that frozen players are freed when another player dribbles a ball between their legs.

Cool-Down

Without an it have players dive through the legs of three different players. When all players have completed their dives the team is dismissed.

99. Five-Pass Volleyball

Number of players	Experience	Playing area
2 teams of 6	Expert	Volleyball court

Recommended Equipment
Volleyball court with a net and one volleyball.

Setup
Place six or more players on either side of the net.

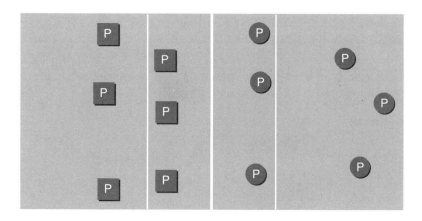

Key Objective
To score points by making the ball land on the opponent's court.

How to Play
Determine which team has first serve by tossing a coin. The server stands behind the backcourt line and serves the ball into the opposition's court. The game continues using regular volleyball rules with the exception that five different players must pass the ball to each other before the sixth player attacks the ball by hitting it over the net. Players may not

➤ carry or throw the ball,

➤ touch the ball twice in a row, or

➤ touch the net.

If the ball goes out of bounds off a player, lands on the court, or is not returned successfully with five passes, the other team scores a point and serves the ball. The first team to reach 25 points (or other preset number of points) wins.

Safety Considerations

Encourage players to be aware of each other (keeping their heads up and calling the balls they are going for) so that they do not bump into each other. Be sure that poles are padded.

Instructional Tips

Students need to communicate with each other to determine who still needs to pass the ball. Remind players to spread themselves out on defense to fill the court and to look for the open areas on offense to score.

Variation

Ten Pass: Allow players to contact the ball more than once (but not twice in a row) per side. All players on the offensive team must contact the ball at least once. Allow as many as 10 passes before the ball must go over the net.

Cool-Down

This game can work well as a cool-down by limiting the serve to an underhand serve and restricting the eventual attack to an overhead pass (set) or forearm pass (bump). No spikes are permitted.

100. Short Volleyball

Number of players	Experience	Playing area
2 teams of 2	Expert	Volleyball court

Recommended Equipment
Volleyball court with a net and one volleyball per group.

Setup
Place two players on the playing court on either side of the net. The court is delineated by a backcourt line (the attack line 9 feet, 10 inches or 3 meters from the net) and two sidelines approximately 3 yards or meters apart. This setup permits as many as three courts (A, B, and C) side by side.

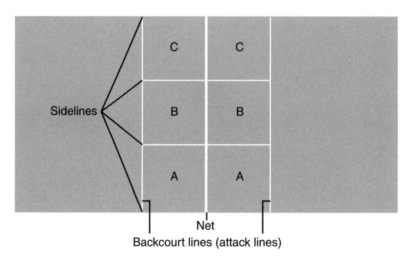

Backcourt lines (attack lines)

Key Objective
To score points by making the ball land on the opponent's court.

How to Play
Determine which team has first serve by tossing a coin. The server stands behind the backcourt line (attack line) and serves the ball into the opposition's court. The game continues using regular volleyball rules. A player may not

- carry or throw the ball,
- touch the ball twice in a row, or
- touch the net.

If the ball goes out of bounds off a player, lands on the court, or is not returned successfully with three or fewer hits, the other team scores a point and serves the ball. The first team to 5 points (or other preset number of points) wins.

Safety Considerations
If three courts are used side by side, warn players to avoid bumping into neighboring players. Have them call a replay if they have any fear of contacting another player when playing a ball.

Instructional Tips
Have players switch courts when any team announces that they have scored 5 points. Winners move one court toward court A, losers move one court toward court C, and the ones at the end stay. (If two teams are tied at that time, the team that reached that point total first is the winner.)

Variations
- **Long and Narrow:** Players play the same game but use the regular back line on the volleyball court.
- **One-on-One:** Players can play either Short Volleyball or Long and Narrow with one player on a side. The player can touch the ball three times before passing the ball over the net on the third hit.

Cool-Down
This game works well as a cool-down, and it is especially useful if some players need to leave. A few players can carry on a little longer with this game after practice.

101. Continuous Pass

Number of players	Experience	Playing area
12 or more	Expert	Volleyball court

Recommended Equipment
Volleyball court with a net and one volleyball.

Setup
Place players on the court as indicated. Player 1 (P1) starts with the ball.

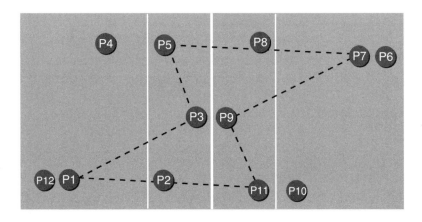

Key Objective
To pass the ball to the desired positions without letting it touch the floor.

How to Play
P1 passes the ball to P3, who passes to P5, who passes to P7, who passes to P9, and so on. After a player has passed the ball she must take the position of the player ahead of her. In other words, P1 passes the ball and then stands where P2 is; P3 passes the ball and goes where P4 is. In the meantime, P12 moves to the spot vacated by P1 and will be the next player in that position to pass the ball; P2 moves to the spot vacated by P3 and will be the next player in that position to pass the ball. Count how many consecutive times players can pass the ball successfully through the six-pass rotation.

Safety Considerations

After players have passed the ball over the net they should go around the post, not under the net, to move to their new position at the end of the court. Be sure that posts are properly padded.

Instructional Tips

All players must have good passing skills for this activity to work successfully. If you have more than 12 players add players at the various positions (this makes the game a little easier because players do not have to move to their new position as quickly).

Variation

Two-Ball Continuous Pass: P1 and P7 each start with a ball in opposite corners. They begin their passes at the same time. This demanding game requires skilled players.

Cool-Down

This game works wonderfully as a cool-down if the challenge is limited to one ball. The group should attempt to go around the complete rotation six times.

REFERENCES

1. Aitken, P. (1997). Basketball. *Physical Education Digest.* Spring, 8-9.

2. Alter, M.J. (2004). *Science of Flexibility* (3rd ed.). Champaign, IL: Human Kinetics.

3. Annesi, J.J. (2002). Effects of differing durations and intensities of cardiovascular exercise on aversion and feeling states in new women exercisers. *Perceptual and Motor Skills.* 94, 735-738.

4. Anshel, M.H. (1985). The effect of arousal on warm-up decrement. *Research Quarterly for Exercise and Sport.* 56, 1-9.

5. Anshel, M.H., and C.A. Wrisberg. (1988). The effect of arousal and focused attention on warm-up decrement. *Journal of Sport Behaviour.* 11, 18-31.

6. Arnett, M.G. (2000). The effect of a morning and afternoon practice schedule on morning and afternoon swim performance. *Journal of Strength and Conditioning Research.* 15, 127-131.

7. Arnett, M.G. (2002). Effects of prolonged and reduced warm-ups on diurnal variation in body temperature and swim performance. *Journal of Strength and Conditioning Research.* 16(2), 256-261.

8. Åstrand, P.O., and K. Rodahl. (1986). *Textbook of Work Physiology.* New York: McGraw-Hill.

9. Atkinson, G., and T. Reilly. (1996). Circadian variation in sports performance. *Sports Medicine.* 21, 292-312.

10. Avela, J.E. (1981). Developing a stretching program. *Physician and Sports Medicine.* 9(11), 59-66.

11. Bandy, W.D., and J.M. Irion. (1994). The effect of time on static stretch on the flexibility of the hamstring muscle. *Physiological Therapy.* 74, 845-852.

12. Baxter, C., and T. Reilly. (1983). Influence of time and day on all-out swimming. *British Journal of Sports Medicine.* 17, 122-127.

13. Bell, G.J., G.D. Snydmiller, D.S. Davies, and A.H. Quinney. (1997). Relationship between aerobic fitness and metabolic recovery from intermittent exercise in endurance athletes. *Canadian Journal of Applied Physiology.* 22(1), 78-85.

14. Bennett, A.F. (1984). Thermal dependence of muscle function. *American Journal of Physiology.* 247, R217-R229.

15. Bishop, D., D. Bonnetti, and B. Lawson. (2000). The effect of three different warm-up intensities on kayak ergometer performance. *Medicine and Science in Sports and Exercise.* 33(6), 1026-1032.

16. Borms, J., P. VanRoy, J.P. Santens, and A. Haentjens. (1971). Optimal duration of static stretching exercises for improvement of coxofemoral flexibility. *Journal of Sports Science.* 5, 39-47.

17. Brehm, B.A. (1987). The warm-up: Its physiological contribution to safe and effective exercise. *Fitness Management.* (November/December), 19-20.

18. Brooks, D.S. (1998). *A Physiological Basis for Warm-Up and Cool Down*. Champaign, IL: Human Kinetics, 153-161.

19. Burkett, L.N., J. Ziuraitis, and W.T. Phillips. (2001). The effect of four different warm-ups on the maximum vertical jump test scores for female college athletes. *Women in Sport and Physical Activity Journal*. 10(2), 83-91.

20. Callaghan, J.P., and S.M. McGill. (2001). Low back joint loading and kinematics during standing and unsupported sitting. *Ergonomics*. 44, 280-294.

21. Cerretelli, P., D. Pendergast, W.C. Pagenelli, and D.W. Rennie. (1979). Effects of specific muscle training on $\dot{V}O_2$ on-response and early blood lactate. *Journal of Applied Physiology*. 47, 761-769.

22. Chu, D.A. (1996). *Explosive Power & Strength*. Champaign, IL: Human Kinetics.

23. Church, B.J., M.S. Wiggins, F.M. Moode, and R. Crist. (2001). Effect of warm-up and flexibility treatments on vertical jump performance. *Journal of Strength and Conditioning Research*. 15(3), 332-336.

24. Coleman, G. (2000). *52-Week Baseball Training*. Champaign, IL: Human Kinetics, 147-156.

25. Cornwell, A., A.G. Nelson, and B. Sidaway. (1999). Acute effects of passive stretching on the neuromechanical behaviour of the triceps surae muscle complex [Abstract]. *Medicine and Science in Sports and Exercise*. 31, S221.

26. Csikszentmihalyi, M. (1990). *Flow: The Psychology of Optimal Experience*. New York: Harper and Row.

27. Davies, C.T.M., I.K. Mecrow, and M.J. White. (1982). Contractile properties of the human triceps surae with some observations on the effects of temperature and exercise. *European Journal of Applied Physiology*. 49, 255-269.

28. Dean, M. (1998). Funky cool down. *Network*. 11(4), 32-33.

29. DeBruyn-Prevost, P., and F. Lefebvre. (1980). The effects of various warming up intensities and durations during a short maximal anaerobic exercise. *European Journal of Applied Physiology*. 29, 101-107.

30. deVries, H.A. (1963). The "looseness" factor in speed and O_2 consumption of an anaerobic 100-yard dash. *Research Quarterly for Exercise and Sport*. 34, 305-313.

31. deVries, H.A. (1974). *Physiology of Exercise*. Dubuque, IA: Brown.

32. deVries, H.A., and T.J. Housh. (1994). *Physiology of Exercise for Physical Education, Athletics, and Exercise Science*. Madison, WI: WCB, Brown & Benchmark.

33. Di Prampero, E., C.T.M. Davies, P. Cerretelli, and R. Margaria. (1970). An analysis of O_2 debt contracted in submaximal exercise. *Journal of Applied Physiology*. 29, 547-551.

34. Di Prampero, P.E., P.B. Mahler, D. Giezendanner, and P. Cerretelli. (1989). Effects of priming exercise on O_2 kinetics and O_2 deficit at the onset of stepping and cycling. *Journal of Applied Physiology*. 66, 2023-2031.

35. Douthitt, B.L. (1994). Psychological determinants of adolescent exercise adherence. *Adolescence*. 29(115), 711-722.

36. Edwards, A.M., N.V. Chalis, J.H. Chapman, D.B. Claxton, and M.L. Fysh. (1999). $\dot{V}O_2$ kinetics determined by PRBS techniques differentiate elite endurance runners from elite sprinters. *International Journal of Sports Medicine.* 20, 1-6.

37. Etnyre, B.R., and E.J. Lee. (1988). Chronic and acute flexibility of men and women using three different stretching techniques. *Research Quarterly for Exercise and Sport.* 59, 222-228.

38. Flanders, J. (1998). Preparing the pitcher for a start. *Coach and Athletic Director.* 68(4), 46-49.

39. Foss, M.L., and S.J. Keteyian. (1998). *Fox's Physiological Basis for Exercise and Sport.* Boston: WCB/McGraw-Hill.

40. Fowles, J.R., and D.G. Sale. (1997). Time course of strength deficit after maximal passive stretch in humans [Abstract]. *Medicine and Science in Sports and Exercise.* 29, S26.

41. Frymoyer, J.W., M.H. Pope, M.C. Costanza, J.C. Rosen, J.E. Goggin, and D.G. Wilder. (1980). Epidemiological studies on low-back pain. *Spine.* 5, 419-423.

42. Gerbino, A., S. Ward, and B. Whipp. (1996). Effects of prior exercise on pulmonary gas-exchange kinetics during high-intensity exercise in humans. *Journal of Applied Physiology.* 80, 99-107.

43. Gleim, G.W., and M.P. McHugh. (1997). Flexibility and its effects on sports injury and performance. *Sports Medicine.* 24, 289-299.

44. Godin, G. (1987). Importance of the emotional aspect of attitude to predict intention. *Psychological Reports.* 61, 719-723.

45. Gray, S., and M. Nimmo. (2001). Effects of active, passive, or no warm-up on metabolism and performance during high intensity exercise. *Journal of Sports Sciences.* 19, 693-700.

46. Green, J.P., S.G. Grenier, and S.M. McGill. (2002). Low-back stiffness is altered with warm-up and bench rest: Implications for athletes. *Medicine and Science in Sports and Exercise.* 34(7), 1076-1081.

47. Guillory, I.K., A.G. Nelson, A. Cromwell, and J. Kokkonen. (1998). Inhibition of maximal torque production by acute stretching is velocity specific [Abstract]. *Medicine and Science in Sports and Exercise.* 30, S101.

48. Gutin, B., K. Stewart, S. Lewis, and J. Kruper. (1976). Oxygen consumption in the first stages of strenuous work as a function of prior exercise. *Journal of Sports Medicine and Physical Fitness.* 16, 60-65.

49. Harris, J., and J. Elbourn. (2002). *Warming Up and Cooling Down* (2nd ed.). Champaign, IL: Human Kinetics.

50. Henderson, K., M. Glancy, and S. Little. (1999). Putting the fun into physical activity. *Journal of Physical Education, Recreation and Dance.* 70(8), 43-49.

51. High, D., and E. Howley. (1989). The effects of static stretching and warm-up on prevention of delayed-onset muscle soreness. *Research Quarterly for Exercise and Sport.* 60(4), 357-361.

52. Holt, J., L.E. Holt, and T.W. Pelham. (1996). Flexibility redefined. In T. Bauer (Ed.), *Biomechanics in Sports XIII*, 170-174. Thunder Bay, ON: Lakehead University.

53. Howe, C.Z., and A.M. Rancourt. (1990). The importance of definitions of selected concepts for leisure inquiry. *Leisure Sciences.* 12, 395-406.

54. Hoyle, R.J., and R.F. Smith. (1989). Warm-up with skill. *Journal of Physical Education, Recreation and Dance.* 60(9), 15-16.

55. Hume, P.A., and J.R. Steele. (2000). A preliminary investigation of injury prevention strategies in netball: Are players heeding the advice? *Journal of Science and Medicine in Sport.* 3(4), 406-413.

56. Hutton, R.S. (1992). Neuromuscular basis of stretching exercises. In P.W. Komi (Ed.), *Biomechanics in Sports XXII*, 170-174. Thunder Bay, ON: Lakehead University.

57. Inbar, O., and O. Bar-Or. (1975). The effects of intermittent warm-up on 7- to 9-year old boys. *European Journal of Applied Physiology.* 34, 81-89.

58. Kerr, J.H. (1989). Anxiety, arousal, and sport performance: An application of reversal theory. In D. Hackfort and C.D. Spielberger (Eds.). *Anxiety in Sports: An International Perspective*, 137-151. New York: Hemisphere.

59. Kokkonen, J., A.G. Nelson, and A. Cornwell. (1998). Acute muscle stretching inhibits maximal strength performance. *Research Quarterly for Exercise and Sport.* 69, 411-415.

60. Knapik, J.J., B.H. Jones, C.L. Bauman, and J. Harris. (1992). Strength, flexibility, and athletic injuries. *Sports Medicine.* 14, 277-288.

61. Knudson, D. (1998). Stretching: From science to practice. *Journal of Physical Education, Recreation and Dance.* 69(3), 38-41.

62. Knudson, D. (1999). Stretching during warm-up. *Journal of Physical Education, Recreation, and Dance.* 70(7), 24-26.

63. Knudson, D., K. Bennett, R. Corn, D. Leick, and C. Smith. (2001). Acute effects of stretching are not evident in the kinematics of the vertical jump. *Journal of Strength and Conditioning Research.* 15(1), 98-101.

64. Krag, M.H., R.E. Seroussi, D.G. Wilder, and M.H. Pope. (1987). Internal displacement distribution from in vitro loading of human thoracic and lumbar spinal motion segments: Experimental results and theoretical predictions. *Spine.* 12, 1001-1007.

65. Lauffenburger, S.K. (1992). Creating a warm-up that works. *Journal of Physical Education, Recreation and Dance.* 63(4), 21-25.

66. Magnusson, S.P., E.B. Simonsen, P. Aagaard, and M. Kjaer. (1996). Biomechanical responses to repeated stretches in human hamstring muscle in vivo. *American Journal of Sports Medicine.* 24, 622-628.

67. McGill, S.M., and S. Brown. (1992). Creep response of the lumbar spine to prolonged full flexion. *Clinical Biomechanics.* 7, 43-46.

68. Medeiros, J.M., G.L. Smidt, L.F. Burmeister, and G.L. Soderberg. The influence of isometric exercise and passive stretch on hip joint motion. *Physical Therapy.* 57, 518-522.

69. Mitchell, M.F. (1996). Stretching the content of your warm-up. *Journal of Physical Education, Recreation and Dance.* 67(7), 24-27.

70. Monedaro, J., and B. Donne. (1998). Effect of different interventions after maximal exercise on lactate removal and subsequent performance. Presented at INABIS 1998—5th Internet World Congress on Biomedical Sciences. At McMaster University, Canada, December 7-16.

71. Nacson, J., and R.A. Schmidt. (1971). The activity-set hypothesis for warm-up decrement. *Journal of Motor Behaviour.* 3, 1-15.

72. Nelson, A.G., A. Cornwell, and G.D. Heise. (1996). Acute stretching exercises and vertical jump stored elastic energy [Abstract]. *Medicine and Science in Sports and Exercise.* 28, S156.

73. Nelson, A.G., and J. Kokkonen. (2001). Acute ballistic muscle stretching inhibits maximal strength performance. *Research Quarterly for Exercise and Sport.* 72(2), 415-419.

74. Noland, M.P., and R.H.L. Feldman. (1985). An empirical investigation of leisure exercise behaviour in adult women. *Health Education.* 16(5), 29-34.

75. Noonan, T.J,. T.M. Best, A.J. Seaber, and W.E. Garrett. (1994). Identification of a threshold for skeletal muscle injury. *American Journal of Sports Medicine.* 22, 257-261.

76. O'Brien, B., W. Payne, P. Gastin, and C. Burge. (1997). A comparison of active and passive warm-ups on energy system contribution and performance in moderate heat. *Australian Journal of Science and Medicine in Sport.* 29(4), 106-109.

77. Oweis, P., and W. Spinks. (2001). Biopsychological, affective and cognitive responses to acute physical activity. *Journal of Sports Medicine and Physical Fitness.* 41, 528-538.

78. Pendergast, D., R. Leibowitz, D. Wilson, and P. Cerretelli. (1983). The effect of preceding anaerobic exercise on aerobic and anaerobic work. *European Journal of Applied Physiology.* 52, 29-35.

79. Peters, G. (2001). Overcoming muscle fatigue. *Coach.* 4, 56-60.

80. Plowman, S.A., and D.L. Smith. (1997). *Exercise Physiology for Health, Fitness, and Performance.* Boston: Allyn and Bacon.

81. Pollock, M.J., G.A. Gaesser, J.D. Butcher, J-P. Despres, R.K. Dishman, B.A. Franklin, and C. Ewing-Garber. (1998). The recommended quantity and quality of exercise for developing and maintaining cardiorespiratory and muscular fitness and flexibility in healthy adults. *Medicine and Science in Sports and Exercise.* 30(6), 975-991.

82. Pope, R.P., R.D. Herbert, J.D. Kirwan, and B.J. Graham. (2000). A randomized trial of pre-exercise stretching for prevention of lower-limb injury. *Medicine and Science in Sports and Exercise.* 32(2), 271-277.

83. Powers, S.K., and E.T. Howley. (2001). *Exercise Physiology: Theory and Application to Fitness and Performance.* New York: McGraw-Hill.

84. Prentice, W.E. (1983). A comparison of static stretching and PNF stretching for improving hip joint flexibility. *Athletic Training.* 18(1), 56-59.

85. Reilly, T., and G.A. Brooks. (1986). Exercise and the circadian variation in body temperature measures. *International Journal of Sports Medicine*. 7, 358-362.

86. Rentström, P., and P. Kannus. (1992). Prevention of injuries in endurance athletes. In R.J. Shephard and P.O. Astrand (Eds.), *Endurance in Sport*. Oxford: Blackwell Scientific.

87. Robergs, R.A., D.D. Pascoe, D.L. Costill, W.J. Fink, J. Chwalbinska-Moneta, J.A. Davis, and R. Hickner. (1991). Effects of warm-up on muscle glycogenolysis during intense exercise. *Medicine and Science in Sports and Exercise*. 23(1), 37-43.

88. Robergs, R.A., and S.O. Roberts. (1997). *Exercise Physiology: Exercise, Performance, and Clinical Applications*. St. Louis: Mosby.

89. Roberts, P. (1995). Goofing. *Psychology Today*. 28(4), 34-41.

90. Rosenbaum, D., and E. Hennig. (1995). The influence of stretching and warm-up exercises on Achilles tendon reflex activity. *Journal of Sports Science*. 13, 481-490.

91. Sady, S.P., M. Wortman, and D. Blanke. (1982). Flexibility training: Ballistic, static, or proprioceptive neuromuscular facilitation? *Archives of Physical Medicine and Rehabilitation*. 63, 261-263.

92. Safran, M.R., A.V. Seaber, and W.E. Garrett. (1989).Warm-up and muscular injury prevention: An update. *Sports Medicine*. 8, 239-249.

93. Sapega, A.A., T.C. Quedenfeld, R.A. Moyer, and R.A. Butler. (1981). Bio-physical factors in range-of-motion exercise. *Physician and Sportsmedicine*. 12(9), 57-65.

94. Shaw, S.M., A. Bonen, and J.F. McCabe. (1991). Do more constraints mean less leisure? Examining the relationship between constraints and participation. *Journal of Leisure Research*. 25, 286-300.

95. Smith, C.A. (1994). The warm-up procedure: To stretch or not to stretch. A brief review. *Journal of Orthopaedic and Sports Physical Therapy*. 19, 12-17.

96. Steinhardt, M.A., and R.K. Dishman. (1989). Reliability and validity of expected outcomes and barriers for habitual physical activity. *Journal of Occupational Medicine*. 31, 536-546.

97. Stephens, M. (2001). Creative cool downs. *Australian Fitness Network*. Special Issue, 58-60.

98. Stewart, I.B., and G.G. Sleivert. (1998). The effect of warm-up intensity on range of motion and anaerobic performance. *Journal of Orthopaedic and Sports Physical Therapy*. 27, 154-161.

99. Surburg, P.R. (1983). Flexibility exercises re-examined. *Athletic Training*. 18, 37-40.

100. Sweet, S., and P. Hagerman. (2001). Warm-up or no warm-up. *Strength and Conditioning Journal*. 23(6), 36.

101. Thomas, M. (2000). The functional warm-up. *Strength and Conditioning Journal*. 22(2), 51-53.

102. Wrisberg, C., and M. Anshel. (1993). The field test of the activity-set hypothesis for warm-up decrement in an open skill. *Research Quarterly for Exercise and Sport*. 64(1), 39-45.

103. Zatisorsky, V.M. (1995). *Science and Practice of Strength Training*. Champaign, IL: Human Kinetics, 102-106.

ABOUT THE AUTHOR

John Byl, PhD, is a professor of physical education at Redeemer University College in Ancaster, Ontario. Dr. Byl has taught physical education and coached for more than 25 years, and he has authored several books related to games and physical activity. He is president of the Canadian Intramural Recreation Association of Ontario and is the chair of Ontario's Active Living Challenge.

Dr. Byl loves cycling and playing squash and golf. He also enjoys playing games with his family, especially his first grandson, Zachary.